INDIAN POLITY

FOR ALL GOVT EXAMS

AWARI SIMANCHAL

Copyright © Awari Simanchal
All Rights Reserved.

This book has been published with all efforts taken to make the material error-free after the consent of the author. However, the author and the publisher do not assume and hereby disclaim any liability to any party for any loss, damage, or disruption caused by errors or omissions, whether such errors or omissions result from negligence, accident, or any other cause.

While every effort has been made to avoid any mistake or omission, this publication is being sold on the condition and understanding that neither the author nor the publishers or printers would be liable in any manner to any person by reason of any mistake or omission in this publication or for any action taken or omitted to be taken or advice rendered or accepted on the basis of this work. For any defect in printing or binding the publishers will be liable only to replace the defective copy by another copy of this work then available.

Contents

CHAPTER ONE

Historical Bsckground Of indian Polity

Indian democracy is a Parliamentary form of democracy where the executive is responsible to the Parliament. The Parliament has two houses – Loksabha and Rajyasabha. Also, the type of governance is Federal, ie there is separate executive and legislature at Center and States. We also have self-governance at local government levels. All these systems owe their legacy to the British administration. Let us see the historical background of the Indian Constitution and its development through the years.

Regulating Act of 1773

- The first step was taken by the British Parliament to control and regulate the affairs of the East India Company in India.
- It designated the **Governor** of Bengal (Fort William) as the **Governor-General (of Bengal).**
- Warren Hastings became the first Governor-General of Bengal.
- Executive Council of the Governor-General was established (Four members). There was no separate legislative council.
- It subordinated the Governors of Bombay and Madras to the Governor-General of Bengal.
- The Supreme Court was established at Fort William (Calcutta) as the Apex Court in 1774.
- It prohibited servants of the company from engaging in any private trade or accepting bribes from the natives.
- Court of Directors (the governing body of the company) should report its revenue.

Pitt's India Act of 1784

- Distinguished between commercial and political functions of the company.
- Court of Directors for Commercial functions and Board of Control for political affairs.
- Reduced the strength of the Governor General's council to three members.
- Placed the Indian affairs under the direct control of the British Government.
- The companies territories in India were called "the British possession in India".
- Governor's councils were established in Madras and Bombay.

Charter Act of 1813

- The Company's monopoly over Indian trade terminated; Trade with India open to all British subjects.

Charter Act of 1833

- **Governor-General (of Bengal)** became the Governor-General of India.
- First Governor-General of India was Lord William Bentick.
- This was the final step towards centralization in British India.
- Beginning of a Central legislature for India as the act also took away legislative powers of Bombay and Madras provinces.
- The Act ended the activities of the East India Company as a commercial body and it became a purely administrative body.Charter Act of 1853

- **The legislative and executive functions of the Governor-General's Council were separated.**

- 6 members in Central legislative council. Four out of six members were appointed by the provisional governments of Madras, Bombay, Bengal and Agra.
- It introduced a system of open competition as the basis for the recruitment of civil servants of the Company (Indian Civil Service opened for all).

Government of India Act of 1858

- The rule of Company was replaced by the rule of the Crown in India.
- The powers of the British Crown were to be exercised by the Secretary of State for India
- He was assisted by the **Council of India**, having 15 members
- He was vested with complete authority and control over the Indian administration through the Viceroy as his agent
- The Governor-General was made the Viceroy of India.
- Lord Canning was the first Viceroy of India.
- Abolished Board of Control and Court of Directors.

Indian Councils Act of 1861

- It introduced for the first time Indian representation in the institutions like Viceroy's executive+legislative council (non-official). **3 Indians entered the Legislative council.**
- Legislative councils were established in Center and provinces.
- It provided that the Viceroy's Executive Council should have some Indians as the non-official members while transacting the legislative businesses.
- It accorded statutory recognition to the portfolio system.
- Initiated the process of decentralisation by restoring the legislative powers to the Bombay and the Madras Provinces.

India Council Act of 1892

- Introduced indirect elections (nomination).
- Enlarged the size of the legislative councils.
- Enlarged the functions of the Legislative Councils and gave them the power of discussing the Budget and addressing questions to the Executive.

Indian Councils Act of 1909

1. This Act is also known as the Morley- Minto Reforms.
2. Direct elections to legislative councils; first attempt at introducing a representative and popular element.
3. It changed the name of the Central Legislative Council to the Imperial Legislative Council.
4. The member of the Central Legislative Council was increased to 60 from 16.
5. Introduced a system of communal representation for Muslims by accepting the concept of 'separate electorate'.
6. **Indians for the first time in Viceroys executive council.** (Satyendra Prasanna Sinha, as the law member)

Government of India Act of 1919

- This Act is also known as the Montague-Chelmsford Reforms.
- The Central subjects were demarcated and separated from those of the Provincial subjects.
- The scheme of dual governance, 'Dyarchy', was introduced in the Provincial subjects.
- Under the dyarchy system, the provincial subjects were divided into two parts – transferred and reserved. On reserved subjects, Governor was not responsible to the Legislative council.
- The Act introduced, for the first time, **bicameralism at the center.**

- **Legislative Assembly** with 140 members and **Legislative council** with 60 members.
- Direct elections.
- The Act also required that the three of the six members of the Viceroy's Executive Council (other than Commander-in-Chief) were to be Indians.
- Provided for the establishment of the Public Service Commission.

Government of India Act of 1935

- The Act provided for the establishment of an All-India Federation consisting of the Provinces and the Princely States as units, though the envisaged federation never came into being.
- Three Lists: The Act divided the powers between the Centre and the units into items of three lists, namely the Federal List, the Provincial List and the Concurrent List.
- The Federal List for the Centre consisted of 59 items, the Provincial List for the provinces consisted of 54 items and the Concurrent List for both consisted of 36 items
- The residuary powers were vested with the Governor-General.
- The Act abolished the Dyarchy in the Provinces and introduced 'Provincial Autonomy'.
- It provided for the adoption of Dyarchy at the Centre.
- Introduced bicameralism in 6 out of 11 Provinces.
- These six Provinces were Assam, Bengal, Bombay, Bihar, Madras and the United Province.
- Provided for the establishment of Federal Court.
- Abolished the Council of India.

Indian Independence Act of 1947

- It declared India as an Independent and Sovereign State.
- Established responsible Governments at both the Centre and the Provinces.

- Designated the Viceroy India and the provincial Governors as the Constitutional (normal heads).
- It assigned dual functions (Constituent and Legislative) to the Constituent Assembly and declared this dominion legislature as a sovereign body.

Points to be noted

- Laws made before the Charter Act of 1833 were called **Regulations** and those made after are called **Acts.**
- Lord Warren Hastings created the office of District Collector in 1772, but judicial powers were separated from District collector later by Cornwallis.
- From the powerful authorities of unchecked executives, the Indian administration developed into a responsible government answerable to the legislature and people.
- The development of the portfolio system and budget points to the separation of power.
- Lord Mayo's resolution on financial decentralization visualized the development of local self-government institutions in India (1870).
- 1882: Lord Ripon's resolution was hailed as the 'Magna Carta' of local self-government. He is regarded as the 'Father of local self-government in India'.
- 1924: Railway Budget was separated from the General Budget based on the Acworth Committee report (1921).
- From 1773 to 1858, the British tried for the centralization of power. It was from the 1861 Councils act they shifted towards devolution of power with provinces.
- 1833 Charter act was the most important act before the act of 1909.
- Till 1947, the Government of India functioned under the provisions of the 1919 Act only. The provisions of the 1935 Act relating to Federation and Dyarchy were never implemented.
- The Executive Council provided by the 1919 Act continued to advise the Viceroy till 1947. The modern executive (Council of Ministers) owes its legacy to the executive council.

- The Legislative Council and Assembly developed into Rajyasabha and Loksabha after independence.

Making Of Indian Constitution

- The **Constituent Assembly** was formed on the recommendation of the **cabinet mission** in 1946
- The Constituent Assembly held its first meeting on **December 9, 1946**
- **Dr. Sachchidanand Sinha**, the oldest member was elected as the temporary President of the Assembly
- **Dr. Rajendra Prasad** was elected as the First President of the Assembly
- On December 13, 1946 Jawaharlal Nehru moved the historic Objectives Resolution in the Assembly
- The Preamble to the Indian Constitution is based on the _Objectives Resolution', drafted and moved by Pandit Nehru, and adopted by the Constituent Assembly
- Constituent Assembly as the provisional parliament of India from January 26, 1950 till the formation of new Parliament after the first general elections in 1951–52.
- The total expenditure incurred on making the Constitution amounted to 64 lakhs
- The Constitution as adopted on November 26, 1949, contained a Preamble, 395 Articles and 8 Schedules and 22 parts.
- Dr BR Ambedkar known as chief architect of Indian Constitution
- Chairman of the Constitution Drafting Committee is **Dr BR Ambedkar**
- **Prem Behari Narain Raizada** was the calligrapher of the Indian Constitution. The original constitution was handwritten by him in a flowing italic style.

FUNCTIONS OF THE CONSTITUENT ASSEMBLY

- It ratified the India's membership of the Commonwealth in May 1949.
- It adopted the national flag on July 22, 1947.
- It adopted the national anthem on January 24, 1950.
- It adopted the national song on January 24, 1950.

- It elected Dr Rajendra Prasad as the first President of India on January 24, 1950

MAJOR COMMITTEES AND ITS CHAIRMEN

- Union Powers Committee – **Jawaharlal Nehru**
- Union Constitution Committee –**Jawaharlal Nehru**
- Provincial Constitution Committee – **Sardar Patel**
- Drafting Committee – **Dr. B.R. Ambedkar**
- Rules of Procedure Committee – **Dr. Rajendra Prasad**
- States Committee– **Jawaharlal Nehru**
- Steering Committee – **Dr. Rajendra Prasad**

SALIENT FEATURES OF THE CONSTITUTION

- **Longest Written Constitution:** The Indian Constitution is considered to be the longest written constitution in the world. It contains different provisions for states and centre and their inter-relationship. The framers of the Constitution have borrowed provisions from several sources and several other Constitutions of the world.
- **Single Constitution** for both the Centre and the states
- **A unique blend of rigidity and flexibility:** Indian Constitution may be called rigid as well as flexible based on its amending procedure.
- **Article 368** in part XX of the constitution deals with the powers of parliament to amend the constitution and its procedure
- The Supreme Court ruled that the constituent power of Parliament under Article 368 does not enable it to alter the _basic structure' of the Constitution
- The 42nd Amendment Act (1976) known as „**Mini-Constitution** "due to the important and large number of changes made by it in various parts of the Constitution.
- The term **socialist, secular and integrity** added to the Preamble of the Indian Constitution by the **42nd Constitutional Amendment Act of 1976**

- **Parliamentary System of Government**: Parliament controls the functioning of the Council of Ministers, and hence it is called the Parliamentary system.
- India has a Parliamentary Form of Government. India has a Bicameral Legislature with two houses named

Lok Sabha and Rajya Sabha.

- **Single Citizenship**: Indian Constitution has the provision for single citizenship provided by the union and recognized by all the states across India.
- The Indian Constitution is federal and envisages a dual polity (Centre and states) it provides for **only a single citizenship**, that is the Indian citizenship
- **Universal Adult Franchise**: The universal adult franchise, which operates with the principle of _one person one vote.' All Indians who are eighteen years of age or above is entitled to vote in the elections. There is no discrimination in voting rights for the citizens of India based on caste, religion, gender, race or status.
- The **voting age** was reduced to **18 years from 21 years** in 1989 by the 61st Constitutional Amendment Act of 1988
- **Fundamental Duties**: The Fundamental Duties of citizens were added to the Constitution by the 42nd Amendment in 1976 on the recommendation of the **Swaran Singh Committee**
- **The Part IV-A** of the Constitution (which consists of only one Article—51-A) specifies the eleven

Fundamental Duties

- **Fundamental Rights**: The Constitution of India asserts the basic principle that every individual is entitled to enjoy certain essential rights. The provisions for Fundamental Rights are mentioned in Part III of the Indian Constitution.

- **Part III** of the Indian Constitution guarantees six **fundamental rights** to all the citizens

  1. Right to Equality (Articles 14–18),
  2. Right to Freedom (Articles 19–22),
  3. Right against Exploitation (Articles 23–24),
  4. Right to Freedom of Religion (Articles 25–28),
  5. Cultural and Educational Rights (Articles 29–30)
  6. Right to Constitutional Remedies (Article 32)

- Fundamental rights can also be suspended during the operation of a National Emergency except the rights guaranteed by **Articles 20 and 21**
- The **Supreme Court** is a federal court, the highest court of appeal, the guarantor of the fundamental rights of the citizens and the guardian of the Constitution.
- **Federal or Unitary:** India is an indestructible Union with destructible states which means it acquires a unitary character during the time of emergency. The Union is not strictly a federal polity but a quasi-federal polity with some vital elements of unitariness.
- **Directive Principles of State Policy:** One of the unique provisions of the Indian Constitution is the Directive Principles of State Policy. These principles are like directives to the government to implement them for establishing social and economic justice in India.
- **Balancing Parliamentary Supremacy with Judicial Review:** Subject to the provisions of any law made by Parliament or any rules made by the Supreme Court under Article 145, the Supreme Court has the power to review any judgment pronounced or made by it. The independent judiciary in India with the power of judicial review is a prominent feature of our constitution

Other Important Points

- The **73rd and 74th Constitutional Amendment Acts (1992)** have added a third-tier of government.
- The 73rd Amendment Act of 1992 gave constitutional recognition to the panchayats (rural local governments) by adding a new Part IX and a new

Schedule 11 to the Constitution.

- The 74th Amendment Act of 1992 gave constitutional recognition to the municipalities (urban local governments) by adding a new Part IX-A and a new Schedule 12 to the Constitution
- The **constitution of India** provides for a parliamentary form of government
- **Article 74 and 75** deals with the parliamentary system at the Centre and article 163 and 164 in the states
- In 1947, Indian Civil Service (ICS) was replaced by IAS and the Indian Police (IP) was replaced by IPS and were recognised by the Constitution as All-India Services
- In 1966, the **Indian Forest Service (IFS)** was created as the third All-India Service
- **Article 312** of the Constitution authorises the **Parliament** to create new **All-India Services** on the basis of a

Rajya Sabha resolution

- **Article 280** provides for a **Finance Commission** as a quasi-judicial body. It is constituted by the President every fifth year or even earlier

CHAPTER TWO

Fundamental Rights And Duties

The constitution of India commenced on 26th January 1950, however, it was completed on 26th November 1949. It consists of various rights as well as duties that are mandatory for the citizens of India. Being an inseparable part of our constitution, fundamental rights and duties are very well explained in it. There are 6 fundamental rights as well as 11 fundamental duties.

Fundamental Rights of Indian Constitution

Defined in part 3 of the Indian constitution, fundamental rights are the basic human rights of all the citizens of India. They are to be followed by all, irrespective of religion, place of birth, race, creed, gender, or caste. Fundamental rights are enforced by the courts and may possess some specific restrictions. Mentioned below are the 6 important fundamental rights derived from the Indian constitution-

1. **Article 14 – 18: Right to Equality**
2. **Article 19 – 22: Right to Freedom**
3. **Article 23 – 24: Right Against Exploitation**
4. **Article 25 – 28: Right to Freedom of Religion**
5. **Article 29 – 30: Cultural and Educational Rights**
6. **Article 30: 35 Right to Constitutional Remedies**

Article 14 – 18: Right to Equality

These articles discuss the importance of equal rights for all citizens of the country, regardless of caste, class, creed, gender, birthplace, or race. It states that equal opportunities in employment and other areas will be provided.

These articles also fight toward the removal of orthodox practices such as untouchability that have been prevalent in the country.

Article 19 – 22: Right to Freedom

This is one of the country's most significant rights. The Indian constitution guarantees residents of the country freedom in a variety of ways. Given below are the fundamental rights of citizens under this article in the Indian constitution.

- Expression
- Speech
- Assembly without arms
- Practicing any profession
- Residing in any part of the country

Article 23 – 24: Right Against Exploitation

The exploitation of humans and their rights are addressed in these articles. Any activity that encourages child labour, human trafficking or other forms of forced labour is prohibited. This article also prevents the government from imposing any mandatory public service.

Furthermore, the state shall not discriminate against anyone on the basis of caste, creed, gender, or other factors when enforcing such obligations.

Article 25 – 28: Right to Freedom of Religion

Since India is a secular country with people of many different religions and faiths, it is essential that we, as well as the Indian constitution, encourage religious freedom. The state can be restrained from enacting laws that are unconstitutional under these articles. It grants citizens of the country to follow or worship any religion of their choice.

Article 29 – 30: Cultural and Educational Rights

These are the articles that help cultural, religious, and linguistic minorities secure their rights by preserving their heritage and culture. There is supposed to be no official religion in the state. According to these articles, the state has no jurisdiction to discriminate against any educational institution based on the fact that it is operated by a minority group.

Article 30: 35 Right to Constitutional Remedies

These articles bind all of the preceding since this right ensures that none of the other essential rights is violated in any way. Any citizen of the country who believes their rights have been violated has the right to go to court and demand justice. The supreme court also has the power to issue search warrants against activities that it deems improper under these articles.

Fundamental Duties of Indian Citizens

Predominantly defined as the moral obligations of the Indian citizens the fundamental duties mentioned in the Indian constitution propagate a spirit of patriotism as well as promote unity amongst the citizens of the country. We have 11 fundamental duties which are mentioned in part IV-A of the constitution along with the Directive Principles. These duties are a vital part of the Indian constitution but are not enforceable by the law. Unlike fundamental rights, every citizen is suggested to abide by the fundamental duties. Let us now explore the 11 fundamental duties of our constitution-

Directive Principles of State Policy

The directive principles of the state policy entail certain guidelines that are used by the Government to frame laws and regulations. Part 4 of the Indian constitution includes directive principles. As stated in article 37, directive principles are not enforceable by the courts under their respective jurisdiction. To put it in simpler words, directive principles are fundamental principles on which certain guidelines of the government are based. It is mandatory for a state to follow the directive principles that are designed by the law. The directive principles of state policy are established in accordance with the other prominent articles of the constitution of India. Let us now dive into important features of this topic-

Citizenship

Citizenship is the status of a person recognized under law as being a legal member of a sovereign state or belonging to a nation. In India, Articles 5 – 11 of the Constitution deals with the concept of citizenship. The term citizenship entails the enjoyment of full membership of any State in which a citizen has civil and political rights.

This is a very important concept to be understood and read for the IAS exam polity and governance segments. With the recent Citizenship Amendment Bill in the news, the topic of citizenship assumes all the more importance.

First, we discuss all the articles in the Indian Constitution pertaining to citizenship.

Article 5: Citizenship at the commencement of the Constitution

This article talks about citizenship for people at the commencement of the Constitution, i.e. 26th January 1950. Under this, citizenship is conferred upon those **persons who have their domicile in Indian territory and –**

1. Who was born in Indian territory; or
2. Whose either parent was born in Indian territory; or
3. Who has ordinarily been a resident of India for not less than 5 years immediately preceding the commencement of the Constitution.

Article 6: Citizenship of certain persons who have migrated from Pakistan

Any person who has migrated from Pakistan shall be a citizen of India at the time of the commencement of the Constitution if –

1. 1. He or either of his parents or any of his grandparents was born in India as given in the Government of India Act of 1935; and
   2. (a) in case such a person has migrated before July 19th, 1948 and has been ordinarily resident in India since his migration, or

(b) in case such as a person has migrated after July 19th, 1948 and he has been registered as a citizen of India by an officer appointed in that behalf by the government of the Dominion of India on an application made by him thereof to such an officer before the commencement of the Constitution, provided that no person shall be so registered unless he has been resident in India for at least 6 months immediately preceding the date of his application.

Article 7: Citizenship of certain migrants to Pakistan

This article deals with the rights of people who had migrated to Pakistan after March 1, 1947, but subsequently returned to India.

Article 8: Citizenship of certain persons of Indian origin residing outside India

This article deals with the rights of people of Indian origin residing outside India for purposes of employment, marriage, and education.

Article 9

People voluntarily acquiring citizenship of a foreign country will not be citizens of India.

Article 10

Any person who is considered a citizen of India under any of the provisions of this Part shall continue to be citizens and will also be subject to any law made by the Parliament.

Article 11: Parliament to regulate the right of citizenship by law

The Parliament has the right to make any provision concerning the acquisition and termination of citizenship and any other matter relating to citizenship.

Citizenship of India constitutional provisions

- Citizenship in India is governed by Articles 5 – 11 (Part II) of the Constitution.
- The Citizenship Act, 1955 is the legislation dealing with citizenship. This has been amended by the Citizenship (Amendment) Act 1986, the Citizenship (Amendment) Act 1992, the Citizenship (Amendment) Act 2003, and the Citizenship (Amendment) Act, 2005.
- Nationality in India mostly follows the jus sanguinis (citizenship by right of blood) and not jus soli (citizenship by right of birth within the territory).

Citizenship Act, 1955

Citizenship of India can be acquired in the following ways:

1. Citizenship at the commencement of the Constitution
2. Citizenship by birth
3. Citizenship by descent
4. Citizenship by registration
5. Citizenship by naturalization
6. By incorporation of territory (by the Government of India)

- People who were domiciled in India as on 26th November 1949 automatically became citizens of India by virtue of citizenship at the commencement of the Constitution.
- Persons who were born in India on or after 26th January 1950 but before 1st July 1987 are Indian citizens.

- A person born after 1ˢᵗ July 1987 is an Indian citizen if either of the parents was a citizen of India at the time of birth.
- Persons born after 3ʳᵈ December 2004 are Indian citizens if both parents are Indian citizens or if one parent is an Indian citizen and the other is not an illegal migrant at the time of birth.
- Citizenship by birth is not applicable for children of foreign diplomatic personnel and those of enemy aliens.

Termination of Indian Citizenship

Termination of citizenship is possible in three ways according to the Act:

1. **Renunciation:** If any citizen of India who is also a national of another country renounces his Indian citizenship through a declaration in the prescribed manner, he ceases to be an Indian citizen. When a male person ceases to be a citizen of India, every minor child of his also ceases to be a citizen of India. However, such a child may within one year after attaining full age become an Indian citizen by making a declaration of his intention to resume Indian citizenship.
2. **Termination:** Indian citizenship can be terminated if a citizen knowingly or voluntarily adopts the citizenship of any foreign country.
3. **Deprivation:** The government of India can deprive a person of his citizenship in some cases. But this is not applicable for all citizens. It is applicable only in the case of citizens who have acquired the citizenship by registration, naturalization, or only by Article 5 Clause (c) (which is citizenship at commencement for a domicile in India and who has ordinarily been a resident of India for not less than 5 years immediately preceding the commencement of the Constitution).

Persons of Indian Origin (PIO) Card

A person would be eligible for the PIO card if he:

1. Is a person of Indian origin and is a citizen of any country except Pakistan, Sri Lanka, Nepal, Bangladesh, Bhutan, China or Afghanistan, or
2. Has held an Indian passport at any other time or is the spouse of a citizen of India or a person of Indian origin.

PIO cardholders can enter India with the multiple entry feature for fifteen years. They do not need a separate visa.

Overseas Citizen of India (OCI) Card

• 19 •

- OCI Card is for foreign nationals who were eligible for Indian citizenship on 26th January 1950 or was an Indian citizen on or after that date.
- Citizens of Pakistan and Bangladesh are not eligible for OCI Card. An OCI cardholder does not have voting rights.
- OCI is not dual citizenship. OCI cardholders are not Indian citizens.
- The OCI Card is a multipurpose, multiple entry lifelong visa for visiting India.
- Persons with OCI Cards have equal rights as NRIs in terms of financial, educational, and economic matters. But they cannot acquire agricultural land in India.

CHAPTER FOUR

Important Articles

1. **Article No. 1:-** Name and territory of the Union

2. **Article No. 3:-** Formation of new states and alteration of areas, boundaries or names of existing states

3. **Article No. 13:-** Laws inconsistent with or in derogation of the <u>Fundamental Rights</u>

4. <u>**Article No. 14:-**</u> Equality before the law

5. **Article No. 16:-** Equality of opportunity in matters of public employment

6. **Article No. 17:-** Abolition of untouchability

7. **Article No. 19:-** Protection of certain rights regarding freedom of speech, etc.

8. **Article No. 21:-** Protection of life and personal liberty

9. **Article No. 21A:-** Right to elementary education

10. **Article No. 25:-** Freedom of conscience and free profession, practice and propagation of religion

11. **Article No. 30:-** Right of minorities to establish and administer educational institutions

12. **Article No. 31C:-** Saving of laws giving effect to certain <u>Directive Principles</u>

13. **Article No. 32:-** Remedies for enforcement of Fundamental Rights including <u>writs</u>

14. **Article No. 38:-** State to secure a social order for the promotion of the welfare of the people

15. **Article No.40:-** Organisation of village <u>panchayats</u>

16. **Article No. 44:-**<u>Uniform Civil Code</u> for the citizens

17. **Article No. 45:-** Provision for early childhood care and education to children below the age of 6 years.

18. Article No. 46:- Promotion of educational and economic interests of <u>scheduled castes, scheduled tribes</u> and other weaker sections

19. Article No. 50:- Separation of <u>judiciary</u> from the executive

20. Article No. 51:- Promotion of international peace and security

21. Article No. 51A:- <u>Fundamental Duties</u>

22. Article No. 72:- Powers of President to grant pardons, suspend, remit or commute sentences in certain cases

23. Article No. 74:- Council of Ministers to aid and advise the <u>President</u>

24. Article No. 76:-<u>Attorney-General of India</u>

25. Article No. 78:- Duties of the Prime Minister as respects the furnishing of information to the President, etc.

26. Article No. 110:- Definition of Money Bills

27. Article No. 112:-<u>Annual Financial Statement (Budget)</u>

28. Article No. 123:- Power of President to promulgate ordinances during recess of Parliament

29. Article No. 143:- Power of President to consult Supreme Court

30. Article No. 148:- <u>Comptroller and Auditor-General of India</u>

31. Article No. 149:- Duties and powers of the Comptroller and Auditor-General of India

32. Article No. 155:-<u>Appointment of the Governor</u>

33. Article No. 161:- Power of Governor to grant pardons, etc., and to suspend, remit or commute sentences in certain cases

34. Article No. 163:- Council of Ministers to aid and advise the Governor

35. Article No. 165:-<u>Advocate-General of the state</u>
<u>Which British Laws are still used in India</u>

36. Article No. 167:-<u>Duties of Chief Minister</u> with regard to the furnishing of information to the Governor, etc.

37. Article No. 168:- Constitution of Legislatures in the states

38. Article No. 169:- Abolition or creation of Legislative Councils in the states

39. Article No. 170:- Composition of Legislative Assemblies in the states

40. Article No. 171:- Composition of Legislative Councils in the states

41. Article No. 172:- Duration of State Legislatures

42. Article No. 173:- Qualification for membership of the State Legislature

43. Article No. 174:- Sessions of the State Legislature, prorogation and dissolution

44. Article No. 178:- Speakers and Deputy Speaker of the Legislative Assembly

45. Article No. 194:- Powers, privileges, and immunity of Advocate-General

46. Article No. 200:- Assent to bills by the governor (including reservation for President)

47. Article No. 202:-Annual financial statement of the State Legislature

48. Article No. 210:- Language to be used in the State Legislature

49. Article No. 212:- Courts not to inquire into proceedings of the State Legislature

50. Article No. 213:- Power of governor to promulgate ordinances during recess of the State Legislature

51. Article No. 214:-<u>High courts for the states</u>

52. Article No. 217:-Appointment and the conditions of the office of the judge of a High Court

53. Article No. 226:- Power of high courts to issue certain writs

54. Article No. 239AA:- Special provisions with respect to Delhi

55. Article No. 243B:-<u>Constitution of Panchayats</u>

56. Article No. 243C:- Composition of Panchayats

57. Article No. 243G:- Powers, authority and responsibilities of Panchayats

58. Article No. 243K:- Elections to the Panchayats

59. Article No. 249:-Power of Parliament to legislate with respect to a matter in the State List in the national interest

60. Article No. 262:- Adjudication of disputes relating to waters of inter-state rivers or river valleys

61. Article No. 263:- Provisions with respect to an inter-state council

62. Article No. 265:- Taxes not to be imposed save by authority of law

63. Article No. 275:- Grants from the Union to certain states

64. Article No. 280:- <u>Finance Commission</u>

65. Article No. 300:- Suits and proceedings

66. Article No. 300A:- Persons not to be deprived of property save by authority of law (Right to property)

67. Article No. 311:- Dismissal, removal or reduction in rank of persons employed in civil capacities under the Union or a state.

68. Article No. 312:-<u>All-India Services</u>

69. Article No. 315:- Public Service Commission for the Union and for the states

70. Article No. 320:- Functions of Public Service Commissions

71. Article No. 323-A:- Administrative Tribunals

72. Article No. 324:- Superintendence, direction and control of elections to be vested in an Election Commission

73. Article No. 330:- Reservation of seats for scheduled castes and scheduled tribes in the House of the People

74. Article No. 335:- Claims of Scheduled Castes and Scheduled Tribes to services and posts

75. Article No. 352:-Proclamation of Emergency (National Emergency)

76. Article No. 356:- Provisions in case of failure of constitutional machinery in states (President's Rule)

77. Article No. 360:- Provisions as to Financial Emergency.

78. Article No. 365:- Effect of failure to comply with or to give effect to, directions given by the Union (President's Rule)

79. Article No. 368:- Power of Parliament to amend the Constitution and procedure therefor

80. Article No. 370:- Temporary provisions with respect to the state o

Part 1 – Art. 1 to art. 4

- Article 1- Name and territory of the union.
- Article 2 – Admission and Establishment of the new state.
- Article 3 – Formation of new states and alteration of areas, boundaries, and the name of existing states.

Part 2 – Art. 5 to art. 11

- Article 5 – Citizenship at the commencement of the constitution.
- Article 6- Rights of citizenship of a certain person who has migrated to India from Pakistan.
- Article 10- continuance of rights of citizenship.
- Article 11- Parliament to regulate the right of citizenship by law.

Part 3 – Art.12 to art.35

- Article 12- Definition of the state
- Article 13 Laws inconsistent with or in derogation of the fundamental rights.
- Originally, the constitution provided for 7 basic fundamental rights, now there are only six rights, one Right to property U/A 31 was deleted from the list of fundamental rights by 44th amendment act 1978. It made a legal right U/A 300-A in Part XII of the constitution.

Some important Fundamental Rights are:
RIGHT TO EQUALITY: ART. 14 TO ART. 18

- Article 14- Equality before the law.
- Article 15- Prohibition of discrimination on the grounds of religion, race, caste, sex. Or place of birth.
- Article 16- Equality of opportunity in matters of public employment.
- Article 17- Abolition of the untouchability.
- Article 18- Abolition of titles

RIGHT TO FREEDOM: ART. 19 TO ART. 22

- Art.19 guarantees to all the citizens the six rights

1. · (a) Right to freedom of speech and expression.
2. · (b) Right to assemble peacefully and without arms.
3. · (c) Right to form associations or unions.
4. · (d) Right to move freely throughout the territory of India.
5. · (e) Right to reside and settle in any part of the territory of India.
6. · (f) Right to practice any profession or to carry on any occupation, trade, and business.

- Article 20- Protection in respect of conviction for offences.
- Article 21-Protection of life and personal liberty.
- Article 21A – Right to education
- Article 22- Protection against arrest and detention in certain cases.

RIGHT AGAINST EXPLOITATION: ART.23 & ART. 24

- Article 23- Prohibition of traffic in human beings and forced labour.
- Article 24- Prohibition of employment of children in factories and mines under age of 14.

RIGHT TO FREEDOM OF RELIGION: ART.25 TO ART. 28

- Article 25- Freedom of conscience and free profession, practice and propagation of religion.
- Article 26- Freedom to manage religious affairs.
- Article 27- Freedom as to pay taxes for promotion of any particular religion.
- Article 28- Freedom from attending religious instruction.

CULTURAL AND EDUCATIONAL RIGHTS: ART.29 & ART. 30

- Article 29- Protection of interest of minorities.
- Article 30- Right of minorities to establish and administer educational institutions.
- Article 32- Remedies for enforcement of Fundamental Rights.

Part.4 Directive Principal of states Policy: Art 36 to art. 51

- Article 36- Definition
- Article 37- Application of DPSP
- Article 39A- Equal justice and free legal aid
- Article 40- Organisation of village panchayat
- Article 41- Right to work, to education, and to public assistance in certain cases
- Article 43- Living Wages, etc. for Workers.
- Article 43A- Participation of workers in management of industries.
- Article 44- Uniform civil code.(applicable in Goa only)
- Article 45- Provision for free and compulsory education for children.
- Article 46- Promotion of educational and economic interest of scheduled castes, ST, and OBC.

- Article 47-Duty of the state to raise the level of nutrition and the standard of living and to improve public health.
- Article 48-Organisation of agriculture and animal husbandry.
- Article 49- Protection of monuments and places and objects of natural importance.
- Article 50- Separation of judiciary from the executive.
- Article 51- Promotion of international peace and security.

Fundamental Duties: Part IV-A- Art 51A

It contains, originally 10 duties, now it contains 11 duties by 86th amendments act 2002.

Part 5 – Union (52-151)

- Article 52- The President of India
- Article 53- Executive Power of the union.
- Article 54- Election of President
- Article 61- Procedure for Impeachment of the President.
- Article 63- The Vice-president of India.
- Article 64- The Vice-President to be ex-officio chairman the Council of States.
- Article 66-Election of Vice-president.
- Article 72-Pardoning powers of President.
- Article 74- Council of Ministers to aid and advise the President.
- Article 76- Attorney-General for India.
- Article 79- Constitution of Parliament
- Article 80- Composition of Rajya Sabha.
- Article 81- Composition of Lok Sabha.
- Article 83- Duration of Houses of Parliament.
- Article 93- The speakers and Deputy speakers of the house of the people.
- Article 105- Powers, Privileges, etc of the House of Parliament.
- Article 109- Special procedure in respect of money bills
- Article 110- Definition of "Money Bills".
- Article 112- Annual Financial Budget.
- Article 114-Appropriation Bills.

- Article 123- Powers of the President to promulgate Ordinances during recess of parliament.
- Article 124- Establishment of Supreme Court.
- Article 125- Salaries of Judges.
- Article 126- Appointment of acting Chief justice.
- Article 127- Appointment of ad-hoc judges.
- Article 128-Attendance of a retired judge at sitting of the Supreme Court.
- Article 129- Supreme court to be a court of Record.
- Article 130- Seat of the Supreme court.
- Article 136- Special leaves for appeal to the Supreme Court.
- Article 137- Review of judgement or orders by the Supreme court.
- Article 141-Decision of the Supreme Court binding on all the courts.
- Article 148- Comptroller and Auditor- General of India
- Article 149- Duties and Powers of CAG.

Part 6 – States (152-237)

- Article 153- Governors of State
- Article 154- Executive Powers of Governor.
- Article 161- Pardoning powers of the Governor.
- Article 165- Advocate-General of the State.
- Article 213- Power of Governor to promulgate ordinances.
- Article 214- High Courts for states.
- Article 215- High Courts to be a court of record.
- Article 226- Power of High Courts to issue certain writs.
- Article 233- Appointment of District judges.
- Article 235- Control over Sub-ordinate Courts.

Part 7 – 238 – Repealed

Part 8 – 239-242 – Union Territories

Part 9 – 243-243 O – Panchayats

- Article 243A- Gram Sabha
- Article 243B- Constitution of Panchayats

Part 9A – 243 P-243 ZG – Municipalities

Part 9B – 243 ZH-243 ZT- Co-operative Societies

Part 10: Scheduled and Tribal Areas -244

Part 11: Center- State Relations 245 – 263

Part 12: Finance, Property, Contracts and Suits (264 – 300A)

- Article 266- Consolidated Fund and Public Accounts Fund
- Article 267- Contingency Fund of India
- Article 280- Finance Commission
- Article 300-A- Right to property.

Part 13: Trade, Commerce and Intercourse within the territories of India (301-307)

- Article 301-Freedom to trade, commerce, and intercourse.
- Article 302- Power of Parliament to impose restrictions on trade, commerce, and intercourse.

Part 14: Services under Center and State (308-323)

- Article 312- All- India-Service.
- Article 315- Public service commissions for the union and for the states
- Article 320- Functions of Public Service Commission.

Part 14A: Tribunals (323 A – 323 B)

- Article 323A- Administrative Tribunals

Part 15 : Elections (324 – 329)

- Article 324-Superintendence, direction and control of Elections to be vested in an Election Commission.
- Article 325- No person to be ineligible for inclusion in or to claim to be included in a special, electoral roll on grounds of religion, race, caste, or sex.
- Article 326- Elections to the house of the people and to the legislative assemblies of states to be on the basis of adult suffrage.

Part 16: Special Provisions to SC, ST, OBC, Minorities etc (330 -342)

- Article 338- National Commission for the SC, & ST.
- Article 340- Appointment of a commission to investigate the conditions of backward classes.

Part 17: Official Language (343- 351)

- Article 343- Official languages of the Union.
- Article 345- Official languages or languages of states.
- Article 348- Languages to be used in the Supreme Court and in the High Courts.
- Article 351-Directive for development of the Hindi languages.

Part 18: Emergency (352-360)

- Article 352- Proclamation of emergency (National Emergency).
- Article 356- State Emergency (President's Rule)
- Article 360- Financial Emergency

Part 19: Miscellaneous (361-367)

- Article 361- Protection of President and Governors

Part 20: Amendment of Constitution (368)

- Article 368- Powers of Parliaments to amend the constitution.

Part 21: Special, Transitional and Temporary Provisions (369 – 392)

- Article 370 – Special provision of J&K.
- Article 371A – Special provision with respect to the State of Nagaland
- Article 371-J: Special Status for Hyderabad-Karnataka region

Part 22: Short Text, Commencement, Authoritative Text in Hindi and Repeals (392 – 395)

- Article 393 – Short title – This Constitution may be called the Constitution of India.

CHAPTER FIVE

Central Government System

President

The **President of India** is the head of state of the Republic of India. The President is the formal head of the executive, legislature and judiciary of India and is also the commander-in-chief of the Indian Armed Forces.

Although Article 53 of the Constitution of India states that the President can exercise his or her powers directly or by subordinate authority, with few exceptions, all of the executive authority vested in the President are, in practice, exercised by the Council of Ministers (CoM).

ARTICLE 52 : THE PRESIDENT OF INDIA

There shall be a President of India.

ARTICLE 53 : EXECUTIVE POWER OF THE UNION

(1) The executive power of the Union shall be vested in the President and shall be exercised by him either directly or through officers subordinate to him in accordance with this Constitution.

(2) Without prejudice to the generality of the foregoing provision, the supreme command of the Defence Forces of the Union Shall be vested in the President and the exercise thereof shall be regulated by law.

(3) Nothing in this article shall –

(a) be deemed to transfer to the President any functions conferred by any existing law on the Government of any State or other authority;or

(b) prevent Parliament from conferring by law functions on authorities other than the President.

ARTICLE 54 : ELECTION OF PRESIDENT

The President shall be elected by the members of an electoral college consisting of –

(a) the elected members of both Houses of Parliament; and

(b) the elected members of the Legislative Assemblies of the States. Explanation: In this article and in article 55, "State" includes the National

Capital Territory of Delhi and the Union territory of Pondicherry.

ARTICLE 55 : MANNER OF ELECTION OF PRESIDENT

(1) As far as practicable, there shall be uniformity in the scale of representation of the different States at the election of the President.

(2) For the purpose of securing such uniformity among the States inter se as well as parity between the States as a whole and the Union, the number of votes which each elected member of Parliament and of the legislative Assembly of each state is entitled to cast at such election shall be determined in the following manner; –

(a) every elected member of the Legislative Assembly of a State shall have as many votes as there are multiples of one thousand in the quotient obtained by dividing the population of the State by the total number of the elected members of the Assembly;

(b) if, after taking the said multiples of one thousand, the remainder is not less than five hundred, then the vote of each member referred to in sub-clause (a) shall be further increased by one;

(c) each elected member of either House of Parliament shall have such number of votes as may be obtained by dividing the total number of votes assigned to the members of the Legislative Assemblies of the States under sub-clauses (a) and (b) by the total number of the elected members of both Houses of Parliament, fractions exceeding one-half being counted as one and other fractionsbeingdisregarded.

(3) The election of the President shall be held in accordance with the system of proportional representation by means of the single transferable vote and the voting at such election shall be by secret ballot.

Explanation: In this article, the expression "population" means the population as ascertained at the last preceding census of which the relevant figures have been published:

Provided that the reference in this Explanation to the last preceding census of which the relevant figures have been published shall, until the relevant figures for the first census taken after the year 2000 have been published, be construed as a reference to the 1971 census.

ARTICLE 56 : TERM OF OFFICE OF PRESIDENT

(1) The President shall hold office for a term of five years from the date on which he enters upon his office:

Provided that – (a) the President may, by writing under his hand addressed to the Vice-President, resign his office;

(b) the President may, for violation of the Constitution, be removed from office by impeachment in the manner provided in article 61.

(c) the President shall, notwithstanding the expiration of his term, continue to hold office until his successor enters upon his office.

(2) Any resignation addressed to the Vice-President under clause (a) of the proviso to clause (1) shall forthwith be communicated by him to the Speaker of the House of the People.

ARTICLE 57 : ELIGIBILITY FOR RE-ELECTION

A person who holds, or who has held, office as President shall, subject to the other provisions of this Constitution be eligible for re-election to that office.

ARTICLE 58 : QUALIFICATIONS FOR ELECTION AS PRESIDENT

(1) No person shall be eligible for election as President unless he –

(a) is a citizen of India;

(b) has completed the age of thirty-five years, and

(c) is qualified for election as a member of the House of the People.

(2) A person shall not be eligible for election as President if he holds any office of profit under the Government of India or the Government of any State or under any local or other authority subject to the control of any of the said Governments.

Explanation: For the purposes of this article, a person shall not be deemed to hold any office of profit by reason only that he is the President or Vice-President of the Union or the Governor of any State or is a Minister either for the Union or for any State.

ARTICLE 59 : CONDITIONS OF PRESIDENT'S OFFICE

(1) The President shall not be a member of either House of Parliament or of a House of the Legislature of any State, and if a member of either House of Parliament or of a House of the Legislature of any State be elected President, he shall be deemed to have vacated his seat in that House on the date on which he enters upon his office as President.

(2) The President shall not hold any other office of profit.

(3) The President shall be entitled without payment of rent to the use of his official residences and shall be also entitled to such emoluments, allowances and privileges as may be determined by Parliament by law and until provision in that behalf is so made, such emoluments, allowances and privileges as are specified in the Second Schedule.

(4) The emoluments and allowances of the President shall not be diminished during his term of office.

ARTICLE 60 : OATH OR AFFIRMATION BY THE PRESIDENT

Every President and every person acting as President or discharging the functions of the President shall, before entering upon his office, make and subscribe in the presence of the Chief Justice of India or, in his absence, the senior most Judge of the Supreme Court available, an oath or affirmation in the following form, that is to say – "I, A.B., do swear in the name of God / solemnly affirm that I will faithfully execute the office of President (or discharge the function of the President) of India and will to the best of my ability preserve, protect and defend the Constitution and the law and that I will devote myself to the service and well-being of the people of India."

ARTICLE 61 : PROCEDURE FOR IMPEACHMENT OF THE PRESIDENT

(1) When a President is to be impeached for violation of the Constitution, the charge shall be preferred by either House of Parliament.

(2) No such charge shall be preferred unless –

(a) the proposal to prefer such charge is contained in a resolution which has been moved after at least fourteen days' notice in writing signed by not less than one-fourth of the total number of members of the House has been given of their intention to move the resolution, and

(b) such resolution has been passed by a majority of not less than two-thirds of the total membership of the House.

(3) When a charge has been so preferred by either House of Parliament, the other House shall investigate the charge or cause the charge to be investigated and the President shall have the right to appear and to be represented at such investigation.

(4) If as a result of the investigation a resolution is passed by a majority of not less than two-thirds of the total membership of the House by which the charge was investigated or caused to be investigated, declaring that the charge preferred against the President has been sustained, such resolution shall have the effect of removing the President from his office as from the date on which the resolution is so passed.

ARTICLE 62 : TIME OF HOLDING ELECTION TO FILL VACANCY IN THE OFFICE OF PRESIDENT AND THE TERM OF OFFICE OR PERSON ELECTED TO FILL CASUAL VACANCY

(1) An election to fill a vacancy caused by the expiration of the term of office of President shall be completed before the expiration of the term.

(2) An election to fill a vacancy in the office of President occurring by reason of his death, resignation or removal, or otherwise shall be held as soon as possible after, and in no case later than six months from, the date of occurrence of the vacancy; and the person elected to fill the vacancy shall,

subject to the provisions of article 56, be entitled to hold office for the full term of five years from the date on which he enters upon his office.

Info-Bits Related to the President of India

1. Salary of Indian President is Rs.5 lakh. Until 2017, the President used to get Rs 1.50 lakh per month. In Budget 2018, it was increased to Rs 5 lakh per month.
2. In addition to the salary, the President receives many other allowances and free facilities which include free medical, housing, and treatment facilities (whole life).
3. The Government of India spends around Rs.2.25 crore rupees annually on other expenses like President's housing, staff, food and hosting of guests.
4. Indian President's salary is 7000$*12=84,000$, which is much lower when compared to US President's salary of 4, 00,000$.
5. The president of the United States of America is also indirectly elected by the people through the Electoral College, but to a four-year term. He is one of only two nationally elected federal officers, the other being the Vice President of the United States. (In total, there are 538 electors, corresponding to the 435 members of the House of Representatives, 100 senators, and the three additional electors from the District of Columbia.)
6. Under The Presidential and Vice-Presidential Elections Act, 1952, a candidate, to be nominated for the office of president of India needs 50 electors as proposers and 50 electors as seconders for his or her name to appear on the ballot.
7. The general principle in Indian Presidential election is that the total number of votes cast by Members of Parliament equals the total number of votes cast by State Legislators.
8. There are a total of 776 voters in both the Houses of Parliament. The Electoral College also consisted of 4120 MLAs in the states.
9. The formula to determine the value of the vote of an MLA = Population of the state ÷ (No. of M.L.A.s in the state X 1000).
10. The formula to determine the value of the vote of an MP = Total value votes assigned to all the M.L.A.s ÷ Total number of MPs.
11. Each MP had a vote value of 708 in the Presidential Election 2012.

12. Legislators from larger states cast more votes than those from smaller states.
13. If a state has few legislators, then each legislator has more votes; if a state has many legislators, then each legislator has fewer votes.
14. JFYI: The President of India moves around in a custom built heavily armoured Mercedes Benz S600 Pullman Guard (which costs around Rs. 12 Crore).
15. Nominated members cannot vote in the Presidential election. But they can participate in President's impeachment.
16. PS: Nominated members can participate in Vice-President's election and removal.
17. MLAs are involved in the Presidential election, but they have no role in President's impeachment. President's impeachment resolution requires a special majority of both houses of the parliament to pass.

Powers of Indian President

Powers of Indian President can be broadly classified under 8 headings. They are :

1. Legislative
2. Executive or Appointment powers
3. Judicial powers
4. Financial powers
5. Diplomatic powers
6. Military powers
7. Pardoning Powers
8. Emergency powers

There are articles outside Chapter 1 of Part V related with powers of President of India like Article 72 and Articles 352-360. We shall discuss in detail each of them later.

Article 72: Power of President to grant pardons, etc., and to suspend, remit or commute sentences in certain cases

(1) The President shall have the power to grant pardons, reprieves, respites or remissions of punishment or to suspend, remit or commute the sentence of any persons convicted of any offence – (a) in all cases where

the punishment of sentence is by a Court Martial;

(b) in all cases where the punishment or sentence is for an offence against any law relating to a matter to which the executive power of theUnionextends;

(c) in all cases where the sentence is a sentence of death.

(2) Nothing in sub-clause (a) of clause (1) shall affect the power conferred by law on any officer of the Armed Forces of the Union to suspend, remit or commute a sentence passed by a Court martial.

(3) Nothing in sub-clause (c) of clause (1) shall affect the power to suspend, remit or commute a sentence of death exercisable by the Governor of a State under any law for the time being in force

Vice President

Part V of the Constitution of India under Chapter I (Executive) also discusses about the office of the Vice-President of India. The Vice-President of India is the second highest constitutional office in the country. He serves for a five-year term, but can continue to be in office, irrespective of the expiry of the term, until the successor assumes office. Let's see the articles 63-73 which deal with the qualifications, election and removal of Vice-President of India.

ARTICLE 63 : THE VICE-PRESIDENT OF INDIA

There shall be a Vice-President of India.

ARTICLE 64 : THE VICE-PRESIDENT TO BE EX-OFFICIO CHAIRMAN OF THE COUNCIL OF STATES

The Vice-President shall be ex-officio Chairman of the Council of States and shall not hold any other office of profit:

Provided that during any period when the Vice-President acts as President or discharges the functions of the President under article 65, he shall not perform the duties of the office of Chairman of the Council of States and shall not be entitled to any salary or allowance payable to the Chairman of the Council of States under article 97.

ARTICLE 65 : THE VICE-PRESIDENT TO ACT AS PRESIDENT OR TO DISCHARGE HIS FUNCTIONS DURING CASUAL VACANCIES IN THE OFFICE, OR DURING THE ABSENCE, OF PRESIDENT

(1) In the event of the occurrence of any vacancy in the office of the President by reason of this death, resignation or removal, or otherwise, the Vice-President shall act as President until the date on which a new President elected in accordance with the provisions of this Chapter to fill such vacancy enters upon his office.

(2) When the President is unable to discharge his functions owing to absence, illness or any other cause, the Vice-President shall discharge his functions until the date on which the President resumes his duties.

(3) The Vice-President shall, during, and in respect of, the period while he is so acting as, or discharging the functions of, President have all the powers and immunities of the President and be entitled to such emoluments, allowances and privileges as may be determined by Parliament by law and, until provision in that behalf is so made, such emoluments, allowances and privileges as are specified in the Second Schedule.

ARTICLE 66 : ELECTION OF VICE-PRESIDENT

(1) The Vice-President shall be elected by the members of an electoral college consisting of the members of both Houses of Parliament in accordance with the system of proportional representation by means of a single transferable vote and the voting at such election shall be by secret ballot.

(2) The Vice-President shall not be a member of either House of Parliament or of a House of the Legislature of any State, and if a member of either House of Parliament or of a House of the Legislature of any State be elected Vice-President, he shall be deemed to have vacated his seat in that House on the date on which he enters upon his office as Vice-President.

(3) No person shall be eligible for election as Vice-President unless he –

(a) is a citizen on India;

(b) has completed the age of thirty-five years; and

(c) is qualified for election as a member of the Council of States.

(4) A person shall not be eligible for election as Vice-President if he holds any office of profit under the Government of India or the Government of any State or under any local or other authority subject to the control of any of the said Governments.

Explanation: For the purposes of this article, a person shall not be deemed to hold any office of profit by reason only that he is the President of Vice-President of the Union or the Governor of any State or is a Minister either for the Union or for any State.

ARTICLE 67 : TERM OF OFFICE OF VICE-PRESIDENT

The Vice-President shall hold office for a term of five years from the date on which he enters upon his office:

Provided that – (a) A Vice-President may, by writing under his hand addressed to the President, resign his office;

(b) a Vice-President may be removed from his office by a resolution of the Council of States passed by a majority of all the then members of the Council and agreed to by the House of the People; but no resolution for the purpose of this clause shall be moved unless at least fourteen days' notice has been given of the intention to move the resolution;

(c) A Vice-President shall, notwithstanding the expiration of his term, continue to hold office until his successor enters upon his office.

ARTICLE 68 : TIME OF HOLDING ELECTION TO FILL VACANCY IN THE OFFICE OF VICE-PRESIDENT AND THE TERM OF OFFICE OF PERSON ELECTED TO FILL CASUAL VACANCY

(1) An election to fill a vacancy caused by the expiration of the term of office of Vice-President shall be completed before the expiration of the term.

(2) An election to fill a vacancy in the office of Vice-President occurring by reason of his death, resignation or removal, or otherwise shall be held as soon as possible after the occurrence of the vacancy, and the person elected to fill the vacancy shall, subject to the provisions of article 67, be entitled to hold office for the full term of five years from the date on which he enters upon his office.

ARTICLE 69 : OATH OR AFFIRMATION BY THE VICE-PRESIDENT

Every Vice-President shall, before entering upon his office, make and subscribe before the President, or some person appointed in that behalf by him, an oath or affirmation in the following form, that is to say – "I, A.B., do swear in the name of God /solemnly affirm that I will bear true faith and allegiance to the Constitution of India as by law established and that I will discharge the duty upon which I am about to enter."

ARTICLE 70 : DISCHARGE OF PRESIDENT'S FUNCTIONS IN OTHER CONTINGENCIES

Parliament may make such provision as it thinks fit for the discharge of the functions of the President in any contingency not provided for in this Chapter.

ARTICLE 71 : MATTERS RELATING TO, OR CONNECTED WITH, THE ELECTION OF A PRESIDENT OR VICE-PRESIDENT

(1) All doubts and disputes arising out of or in connection with the election of a President or Vice-President shall be inquired into and decided by the Supreme Court whose decision shall be final.

(2) If the election of a person as President or Vice-President is declared void by the Supreme Court, acts done by him in the exercise and performance of the powers and duties of the office of President or Vice-President, as the

case may be, on or before the date of the decision of the Supreme Court shall not be invalidated by reason of that declaration.

(3) Subject to the provisions of this Constitution, Parliament may by law regulate any matter relating to or connected with the election of a President or Vice-President.

(4) The election of a person as President or Vice-President shall not be called in question on the ground of the existence of any vacancy for whatever reason among the members of the electoral college electing him.

ARTICLE 72 : POWER OF PRESIDENT TO GRANT PARDONS, ETC., AND TO SUSPEND, REMIT OR COMMUTE SENTENCES IN CERTAIN CASES

(1) The President shall have the power to grant pardons, reprieves, respites or remissions of punishment or to suspend, remit or commute the sentence of any persons convicted of any offence – (a) in all cases where the punishment of sentence is by a Court Martial;

(b) in all cases where the punishment or sentence is for an offence against any law relating to a matter to which the executive power of the Union extends;

(c) in all cases where the sentence is a sentence of death.

(2) Nothing in sub-clause (a) of clause (1) shall affect the power conferred by law on any officer of the Armed Forces of the Union to suspend, remit or commute a sentence passed by a Court martial.

(3) Nothing in sub-clause (c) of clause (1) shall affect the power to suspend, remit or commute a sentence of death exercisable by the Governor of a State under any law for the time being in force.

*ARTICLE 73 : EXTENT OF EXECUTIVE POWER OF THE UNION**

(1) Subject to the provisions of this Constitution, the executive power of the Union shall extend—

(a) to the matters with respect to which Parliament has power to make laws; and

(b) to the exercise of such rights, authority and jurisdiction as are exercisable by the Government of India by virtue of any treaty or agreement:

Provided that the executive power referred to in sub-clause (a) shall not, save as expressly provided in this Constitution or in any law made by Parliament,

extend in any State to matters with respect to which the Legislature of the State has also power to make laws.

(2) Until otherwise provided by Parliament, a State and any officer or authority of a State may, notwithstanding anything in this article, continue to exercise in matters with respect to which Parliament has power to make laws for that State such executive power or functions as the State or officer or authority thereof could exercise immediately before the commencement of this Constitution.

Info-Bits related with the Vice-President of India

The office of the Vice-President of India is special because of multiple reasons. It would be interesting to explore the constitutional provisions related to VP of India. Try, if you can find the answers of the following questions, yourself.

1. Can Vice-President of India continue to be in office irrespective of the expiry of his term of 5 years?
2. Who performs the duties of the Vice-President, when a vacancy occurs in the office of the Vice-President of India, before the expiry of his term?
3. Who performs the duties of the Vice-President, when a vacancy occurs in the office of the Vice-President of India, when the Vice-President acts as the President of India?
4. Who performs the Vice-President's function as the Chairperson of the Council of States (Rajya Sabha) when a vacancy occurs in the office of the Vice-President of India?
5. Salary for Vice-President for his role as Vice-President of India?
6. Salary for Vice-President for his role as ex-officio Chairperson of the Council of States (Rajya Sabha)?
7. Salary for Vice-President when Vice-President acts as President of India?
8. Can nominated members participate in the election and removal process of Vice President?
9. Vice-President is neither an elected nor nominated member of Rajya Sabha. But being the chairman of Rajya Sabha, can he cast vote?
10. How can the Vice-President of India removed from his office?

Answers:

1. Can Vice-President of India continue to be in office irrespective of the expiry of his term of 5 years? **Ans : Yes. Until the successor assumes**

office.

2. Who performs the duties of the Vice-President, when a vacancy occurs in the office of the Vice-President of India, before the expiry of his term? **Ans : Constitution is silent on this matter.**

3. Who performs the duties of the Vice-President, when a vacancy occurs in the office of the Vice-President of India, when the Vice-President acts as the President of India? **Ans : Constitution is silent on this matter.**

4. Who performs the Vice-President's function as the Chairperson of the Council of States (Rajya Sabha) when a vacancy occurs in the office of the Vice-President of India? **Ans : Deputy Chairperson of the Rajya Sabha, or any other member of the Rajya Sabha authorised by the President of India.**

5. Salary for Vice-President for his role as Vice-President of India? **Ans : No salary for the role as Vice-President. Salary is for the role as ex-officio Chairperson of the Council of States (Rajya Sabha).**

6. Salary for Vice-President for his role as ex-officio Chairperson of the Council of States (Rajya Sabha)? **Ans : Rs.1.25 lakhs.**

7. Salary for Vice-President when Vice-President acts as President of India? **Ans : He will get salary of Indian President, ie Rs.1.5 lakh. But he will stop getting the salary of ex-officio chaiman of Rajya Sabha.**

8. Can nominated members participate in the election and removal process of Vice President? **Ans: Yes. (NB: For Presidential election nominated members cannot participate.)**

9. Vice-President is neither an elected nor nominated member of Rajya Sabha. But being the chairman of Rajya Sabha, can he cast vote? **Ans : Yes. The Chairman has a casting vote in the case of an equality of votes.**

10. How can the Vice-President of India removed from his office? **Ans : Vice-President may be removed from his office by a resolution of the Council of States passed by a majority of all the then members of the Council and agreed to by the House of the People; but no resolution for the purpose of this clause shall be moved unless at least fourteen days' notice has been given of the intention to move the resolution.**

Removal of Vice-President of India: Must Check

Aspirants are requested to note a mistake which you might find in many textbooks on Indian Polity, under the topic 'Removal of the Vice-President of India'. I have seen text-books mentioning that removal of Vice-President needs absolute majority (half of the total strength of the house). But this cannot be right.

Prime Minister

To prepare for INDIAN POLITY for any competitive exam, aspirants have to know about the Prime Minister of India. It gives an idea of all the important topics for IAS Exam and the polity syllabus (GS-II.). This is an essential portion of the polity. As IAS aspirants, you should be thorough with the Prime Minister of India. In this article, you can read all about the Prime Minister for the polity and governance segments of the UPSC syllabus. Prime Minister is the head of the Government. He is appointed by the President. He can be a member of either Lok Sabha or Rajya Sabha. President should appoint the leader of the majority party or coalition parties as to the Prime Minister. He acts like a chain between the President and the Council of Ministers. He is the Political head of Civil Servants.

"If any functionary under our constitution is to be compared with the US President, he is the Prime Minister and not the President of the Union" – ***B.R. Ambedkar.***

CONSTITUTIONAL BASIS

- **74-** Council of Ministers to aid and advice VICE – PRESIDENT.
- PM is the **real executive authority (de facto executive)** in parliamentary form of government.(President –Nominal; de jure executive)
- PM is the **head of the government.** (President is the head of the State)

The Constitution **does not** contain any specific procedure for the selection and appointment of the PM. It is by and large, governed by **Parliamentary Conventions.**

Appointment of the PM

- **75** –Says **only** that the **Prime Minister shall be appointed by the President.**
- However, the President is **not free to appoint any one** as the Prime Minister.

- **As per the conventions of parliamentary system** – The President has to appoint the **leader of the majority party in the Lok Sabha** as the Prime Minister.

PERSONAL DISCRETION OF THE PRESIDENT

- When **noparty has a clear majorityin the Lok Sabha**, then the **President may exercise his personal discretion** in the selection and appointment of the PM.
- In such scenario, the President **usually appoints the leader of the largest party or coalition in the Lok Sabha** as the PM and **asks him to seek a vote of confidence in the House within a month.**
- Discretion was exercised first time in **1979,** when the Neelam Sanjiva Reddy (then President) appointed Charan Singh (Coalition leader) as the PM after fall of Morarji Desai's Janta Party Government.
- The president may have to exercise his **individual judgment** in the selection and appointment of the PM, when PM in office **dies suddenly** and there is **no obvious successor.**
- **However, if the ruling party elects a new leader** after the death of an incumbent PM, then the **President has no choice but to appoint** him as PM.
- **Delhi High Court (1980)**à The Constitution **does not require that a person must prove his majority in the Lok Sabha before he is appointed** as the PM.
- The President **may first appoint him the PM** and **then ask him to prove his majority in the Lok Sabha** within a reasonable period.
- **Supreme Court (1997)**à a person who is **not a member of either House of Parliament (i.e. Lok Sabha and Rajya Sabha) can be appointed as PM for six months,** within which, he should become a member of either House of Parliament; **otherwise, he ceases to be the PM.**
- Constitutionally, the **PM may be a member of any of the two Houses of parliament.** For e.g. Indira Gandhi (1966), Deve Gowda (1996) and Manmohan Singh (2004), were members of the Rajya Sabha.

OATH, TERM AND SALARY

- **The President** administers to him the **oaths of office and secrecy.**
- In his oath of office the PM swear

- to bear true **faith and allegiance to the constitution of India.**
- to **uphold sovereignty and integrity of India.**
- to faithfully and conscientiously discharge duties of his office and
- to do right to all people in accordance with the Constitution and the law, without fear, favor or ill will.
- In his oath to secrecy, the PM swear **not to reveal any matter that is brought under his consideration as a Union Minister** except required for due discharge of duties.
- The **term** of the PM is **not fixed** and he holds office during the **pleasure of the President.** However, as long as the **PM enjoys the majority** support in the Lok Sabha, **he cannot be dismissed by the President.**
- In case of **loss of confidence (majority)** of the Lok Sabha, the **PM must resign** or the **President can dismiss him.**
- The salary and allowances of the PM are determined by the **Parliament** from time to time. PM gets the salary and allowances that are **payable to a member of Parliament.**

"Oath of Secrecy" should be replace by "Oath of Transparency" – **Second ARC**

SCHOOLS OF THOUGHTS

- PM as **'primus inter pares'** (first among equals) à PM is more like a coordinating function. For e.g. Coalition PM are close to this school of thought.
- PM as **'inter stellas luna minores'** (a moon among lesser stars)à We have "Prime Ministerial" government instead of "Cabinet Government". For e.g. Jawaharlal Nehru, Indira Gandhi, Rajiv Gandhi, Narendra Modi Government.
- **However, B. Vajpayee** was **notable exception** to both school of thoughts and held as **blend of both schools.**

FACTORS THAT STRENGTHEN THE POSITION OF THE PM IN INDIA

- PM is the chairperson of Cabinet, CoM, important cabinet committees.
- The **resignation or death of an incumbent PM automatically dissolves the CoM** and thereby **generates a vacuum.**

- The **resignation or death of any other minister,** on the other hand, merely creates a **vacancy,** which the PM may or may not like to fill.
- He is the chairperson of high-powered bodies – NITI Aayog, National Integration Council (NIC), Inter-State Councils (ISC), National Water Resource Council etc.
- He is the **chief spokesman** of the Union government.
- He is **leader of the party in power.** PM is generally equated with his party. ("PM is party and Party is PM").
- He is **political head** of the services.
- Support of high-powered bodies – PRIME MINISTER'S OFFICE and Cabinet Secretariat.
- PM becomes leader of house of which he is member.

ROLE OF THE PRIME MINISTER

1. **Role of PM w.r.t. the President**

- PM is the **principal channel of communication** (Art. 78) between the President and the CoM.
- It is the duty of the PM

  - to **communicate to the President all decisions** (Art. 78) of the CoM,
  - to **furnish information** relating to the administration of the affairs of the Union and proposal for legislations as the President may call for and
  - if the President so requires, to **submit for the consideration of the CoM** any matter on which a decision has been taken by a minister but which has not been considered by the council.

- PM **advises the President** with regard to the **appointment of important officials** like Attorney General of India, Comptroller and Auditor General of India, Chairperson and members of UPSC and so on.

1. **Role of the PM w.r.t. the CoM**

  - PM **recommends** persons **who can be appointed as ministers** by the President.

- The **President can appoint only those persons** as ministers who are recommended by the PM.
- He **allocates** and **reshuffles various portfolios** among the ministers.
- He can **ask a minister to resign or advise the President to dismiss** him in case of difference of opinion.
- He **presides over the meeting of CoM** and influences its decisions.
- He **guides, directs, controls** and **coordinates** the activities of all the ministers.
- His death or resignation from office can **bring the collapse of the CoM.**

3. **Role of PM w.r.t. the Parliament**

- - The PM is the **leader of the Lower House (Lok Sabha).**
  - He **advises the President** with regard to **summoning** and **proroguing** of the sessions of the Parliament.
  - He can **recommend dissolution of the Lok Sabha** to President at any time.
  - He **announces government policies** on the floor of the House.

4. **Role of the PM w.r.t. the Cabinet**

- - PM constitute cabinet and allocates portfolios.
  - He summons cabinet meeting and also decides agenda of meeting.
  - It is the PM's privilege to consult any person on any matter he deems fit and it is his discretion to act occasionally without any consultation.

5. **Role of PM w.r.t. the External affairs**

- - This domain has been personally directed by PM.
  - If PM respected by international communities, it can help him acquire greater respect domestically as well.
  - He plays a significant role in shaping the foreign policy of the country.

6. **Role of PM w.r.t. the Planning**

- - He is the **crisis manager-in-chief** at the political level during emergencies.
  - He is Chairperson of National Disaster Management Authority.

7. **Role of PM w.r.t. the CABINET COMMITTEEs**

- - The PM setups Cabinet Committees and are headed by him when he is member.

    - Cabinet Committee on Political Affairs (Known as "Super-Cabinet") – PM
    - Cabinet Committee on Economic Affairs – PM
    - Cabinet Committee on Appointments – PM

RELATIONSHIP OF PM WITH PRESIDENT

- **74**– There shall be a **CoM with the PM at the head to aid and advise the President** who shall, in the exercise of his functions, act in accordance with such advice. However, the **President may require the CoM to reconsider such advice** and the **President shall act in accordance with the advice tendered after such reconsideration** (Added by **44**[th] **amendment act 1978**).
- **75 – The PM shall be appointed by the President** and the **other ministers shall be appointed by the president on the advice of the PM.**

  - The ministers shall hold office during the **pleasure of the president.**
  - The CoM shall be **collectively responsible to the House of the People** (Lok Sabha).

- **78**– It shall be the duty of the PM:

  - to **communicate to the President all decisions** of the CoM relating to the administration of the affairs of the Union and proposals for legislation.
  - to **furnish such information** relating to the administration of the affairs of the Union and proposals for legislation as the President may call for.

- ◦ if the President so requires, **to submit for the consideration of the council of ministers any matter on which a decision has been taken** by a minister but which has not been considered by the CoM.

ARGUMENTS IN FAVOUR OF PRIME MINISTER FROM LOWER HOUSE (LOK SABHA)

- Leader of CoM should be member of Lower house (Lok Sabha) to which CoM is **collectively responsible.**
- Purpose of the **Rajya Sabha is not to produce government** but to ensure representation to state and protect their interests.
- Convention in other parliamentary democracies endorses the same. For e.g.

  - ◦ In **Britain**, PM comes from House of Commons (Lower House).
  - ◦ In **Germany**, federal chancellor comes from lower house (Bundestag).
  - ◦ **Japanese** PM comes from lower house, called as Diet.

- **Nehru** endorse and supported same.
- **V Kamath introduced Constitutional Amendment Bill** (in 1966) to codify the same provision. Congress broadly agreed with the same but held that **it should evolve as convention rather than statute.**

LIST OF CM WHO BECAME PM

- **Morarji Desai-** CM of the erstwhile Bombay State, the first non-Congress PM.
- **Charan Singh-**Was CM of the undivided Uttar Pradesh
- **P. Singh-** Was CM of the Uttar Pradesh
- **V. Narasimha Rao-** first PM from South India, who was CM of Andhra Pradesh
- **D. Deve Gowda-** Was CM of Karnataka.
- **Narendra Modi-** Was four-time CM of Gujarat

Council Of Ministers

The President, Vice-President, Council of Ministers led by the Prime Minister, and Attorney General are all mentioned in Chapter I- Executive of

Part V of the Constitution i.e., Union. Constitution framers have established the British pattern of Cabinet Government in India.

Article 74 of the Constitution provides that there shall be a Council of Ministers with the Prime Minister at the head to aid and advise the President who shall, in the exercise of his functions, act in accordance with such advice. The Council of Ministers is made up of the Prime Minister and other Ministers. Cabinet Ministers, Ministers of State, and Deputy Ministers are the three types of ministers. The President of India appoints each of them. The UPSC Indian Polity and Governance Syllabus includes Council Of Ministers - Union Executive which is described in this article.

Council Of Ministers - Union Executive - Historical Background

- The Indian Constitution has borrowed the British Parliamentary form of Government in which the real executive of the Indian Union is the Council of Ministers headed by the Prime Minister, which actually exercises the executive authority, theoretically vested by the Constitution, in the President.
- **Was started by Lord Canning** in Indian Councils Act 1861.

- **Article 74: Council of Ministers to aid and advice President-**
- Clause (1) there shall be a Council of Ministers with the Prime Minister at the head to aid and advise the President who shall, in the exercise of his functions, act in accordance with such advice:
- **Provided that the President may require the Council of Ministers to reconsider such advice, either generally or otherwise, and the President shall act in accordance with the advice tendered after such reconsideration.**
- Clause (2) the question whether any and if so what, **advice was tendered by Ministers to the President shall not be inquired into in any court.**
- **Article 75(1)** of the Constitution says that "the Prime Minister shall be **appointed by the President and the other Ministers shall be appointed by the President on the advice of the Prime Minister."**

Other Provisions Of Article 75 Are As Follows

- The total number of Ministers, including the Prime Minister, in the **Council of Ministers shall not exceed 15% of the total number of members of the House of the People.**
- The **ministers hold office during the pleasure of the President.**
- The Council of Ministers is **collectively responsible to the House of the People.**
- Before a minister takes over his office, the **President administers to him the oath of office and secrecy** according to the forms set out for the purpose in the third Schedule.
- The **salaries and allowances of ministers are such as the Parliament may from time to time determined by law** and, until Parliament so determines, shall be as specified in the Second Schedule.
- A member of either House of the Parliament belonging to any political party is disqualified for being a member of that house under the 10th Schedule shall also be disqualified to be appointed as a minister under clause (1) for the duration of the period commencing from the date of his disqualification till the date on which the term of his office as such member would expire or where the contests any election to either House of Parliament before the expiry of such period, till the date on which he is declared elected, whichever is earlier.
- A minister who for any period of six consecutive months is not a member of either House of the Parliament shall at the expiration of that period ceases to be a Minister

Formation Of Council Of Ministers

- The process of formation of the Council of Ministers begins with the **appointment of the Prime Minister by the President.**
- While appointing the Prime Minister, the **President will have little opportunity to exercise his own discretion.** He will have to be the **leader of the party which secures a majority** in the Lok Sabha.
- Only when none of the parties represented in the Lok Sabha commands a clear majority, the President may have some discretion within the

bounds of conventions.

- The section of other Ministers, in practice, is entirely the discretion of the Prime Minister. The **President has to simply accept the recommendations of the Prime Minister.**
- The **Prime Minister selects other Ministers**. The President has to accept the team chosen by him.

Qualification Of Council Of Minister

- Minister **must be a member of either House of Parliament.**
- If a person who is **not a member** of either House of the Parliament is appointed as a Minister, **he shall cease to be a minister after six months** unless in the meanwhile Minister has to get himself/herself elected to either House of Parliament within six months.

Disqualification Of Council Of Minister Due To Defection

Also, if a member of Parliament has been disqualified on the ground of defection, he would not be eligible to become a Minister. But if he again gets elected in the next freshly held Parliamentary election then he will be eligible to become a minister.

Participation Of Council Of Minister In Parliamentary Proceeding

- The **Ministers may be chosen from members of either House.**
- A Minister who is a member of one House has a **right to speak in and to take part in the proceedings of the other House though he has no right to vote** in the house of which **he is not a member.**

Salary Of Council Of Minister

The constitution declares that The salaries and allowances of ministers are such as the Parliament may from time to time determined by law. As a result of a law established by Parliament in 1985, each minister is entitled to the same pay and allowances as a member of Parliament.

Strength

Strength Of Council Of Ministers

- Its **size and classification are not mentioned in the Constitution.**
- Its **size is determined by the Prime Minister** according to the exigencies of the time and requirements of the situation.
- But as per **91st Constitutional Amendment Act, 2003, it should not exceed 15%** of the total strength of the Lok Sabha

Term Of Office Of Council Of Ministers

- Ministers are **appointed by the President and remain at his pleasure.** It only signifies something if they continue to have the support of the Lok Sabha's majority. Any minister can be asked to resign by the Prime Minister at any moment, and the latter must obey.
- The **Prime Minister has the authority to suggest the dismissal of any minister to the President,** and the President always follows his advice. When the Prime Minister resigns, the whole Council of Ministers resigns with him.
- As a result, the **ministry's or a minister's tenure is not fixed.** A ministry/each minister continues in office for as long as the majority in the Lok Sabha has confidence in it, or as long as the Prime Minister does not quit.
- The **maximum duration for which a minister can be in office is five years** or one complete Lok Sabha term.
- Even if the same party that won a majority in the previous Lok Sabha returns with a majority in the next Lok Sabha, a new cabinet must be formed after each new general election to the Lok Sabha

Categories Of Ministers

- Council of Ministers is not a single body but a composite body, consisting of ministers of different ranks. The **constitution does not classify the members of the Council of Ministers into different ranks.** The classification is done informally following British practice.
- **Cabinet Minister:**
- They are experienced Ministers who hold very important portfolios like Home, Finance, Defence, Agriculture, Foreign Affairs, etc.
- Their number varies from time to time but it is generally in the range of 15 to 20.
- A Cabinet Minister always heads a Ministry and is given independent charge of it, unless he is appointed a Minister without portfolio. He attends the meeting of the Cabinet on his own right and is generally assisted by a Minister of State or a Deputy Minister or both.

Minister of State

- A Minister of State may be given independent charge of a Ministry.
- He cannot attend the meetings of the Cabinet on his own right but can attend if invited.

Deputy Minister

- A Deputy Minister is a junior member of the Council of Minster and not given independent charge of any department.
- He is put under the charge of either minister of the cabinet rank or that of the Minister of State so that he gets proper training.
- He does not attend a Cabinet meeting

Power Of Council Of Ministers

Executive Power

- The Council of Ministers exercises all of the President of India's executive functions.
- The Cabinet develops the policies that will be presented to Parliament for approval. It obtains Parliamentary approval for these measures and then implements them. It manages the Union's administration in accordance with authorized policies. All government departments are coordinated and controlled by the Cabinet/Prime Minister. The Cabinet is in charge of formulating foreign policy as well as all domestic policies deemed important for the country's overall development.
- The **Council of Ministers is collectively responsible to the Lok Sabha for all of its policies and decisions**. Any failure on any front could lead to the ministry's demise.

Emergency Power

- The **President always acts on the recommendation of the Prime Minister and his Council of Ministers when he exercises Emergency Powers**.
- Only with the Cabinet's approval may the President declare an emergency. In accordance with the Prime Minister's and his Council of Ministers' advice, he takes all necessary steps to address the emergency.

Legislative Power

- Despite the fact that the Union's legislative powers are in the hands of Parliament, the Council of Ministers plays an essential role in the legislative process. Ministers are members of the Parliament as well as heads of government ministries. They participate fully and actively in the legislative process.

- They are the ones who introduce and pilot the majority of the bills. The Parliament spends 95 percent of its time dealing with governmental business, which is overseen by ministers. Because the ministry has the backing of the majority in Parliament, a measure that is not backed by the Council of Ministers cannot be passed.
- If the Lok Sabha passes a bill that the Council of Ministers does not support or rejects a bill that the Council of Ministers supports, or rejects the Cabinet's budget, it is considered a vote of no confidence in the government, and the whole Council of Ministers resigns. While doing so, the Prime Minister/Cabinet might recommend to the President that the Lok Sabha be dissolved

Responsibility Of Council Of Ministers

Collective Responsibility

- The basic principle of Parliamentary or Cabinet form of Government on the principle of collective responsibility. Collective cabinet responsibility refers to the accepted conduct of Government Ministers as a part of the Cabinet. In England, it works on well-established conventions. In India, this principle is ensured by making specific provisions in the Constitution.
- Article 75(3) states that "the Council of Ministers is collectively responsible to the House of the People."
- **Confidence of the House-** A government can remain in office for so long as it retains the confidence of the House of People, confidence which can be assumed unless and until proven otherwise by a confidence vote. So, if a decision of a particular Ministry on a policy matter is defeated in a Lok Sabha, it is not the Minister who resigns, but the whole Council of Ministers resign. The Council of Ministers sinks and swims together. It stands or falls together.
- The individual Minister may have differences among themselves on certain issues, but once a decision is taken by Cabinet, it becomes the joint decision of all the Ministers. It is the duty of each and every Minister to stand by it and support it in Parliament and outside.

- If any minister disagrees with a cabinet decision and is not prepared to defend it, he must resign.
- In 1953, B.R. Ambedkar resigned due to disagreements with his colleagues over the Hindu Code Bill.
- Due to his objection to the Muslim Women (Protection of Rights on Divorce) Act of 1986, Arif Mohammed resigned.
- The basic idea behind the principle of collective responsibility is to provide unity and homogeneity to the Cabinet so that the functioning of the Government is not retarded.

Individual Responsibility

- Though the Ministers are collectively responsible to the Lok Sabha, they shall be individually responsible to the Head of the State i.e., President.
- Article 75(2) declares that the Ministers shall be liable to be removed by the President at any time.
- However, since the President has to act on the advice of the Prime Minister, in practice, this power is exercised by the Prime Minister. The Prime Minister ask the Minister to resign.

No Legal Responsibility

- The system of legal responsibility is not prescribed in the Indian Constitution.
- In the UK the monarch cannot do any public act without the counter signature of a minister who is legally responsible for the act. If the act violates the law, the minister is responsible in a court of law.
- In India, an order of the President for a public act should not be countersigned by a minister. It is left to the President to make rules as to how his orders are to be authenticated.
- Further the courts are barred from inquiring into the nature of advice rendered by the ministers.

Position of the Council of Ministers

- In the Indian political system, the Council of Ministers has a significant and central role as the real and powerful executive.
- The Council of Ministers really exercises all of the President of India's powers.
- The Cabinet is the most powerful entity in the Council of Ministers. All of these powers are exercised by the central institution. The Cabinet is in charge of directing, supervising, and controlling the creation of national policies as well as the administration's operations.
- As the maker of all policies, the director of administration and the supreme coordinator of government activity, the Cabinet enjoys an enviable position. It is indeed the steering wheel of the ship of the state. It is the centre of power and the most powerful institution of the Indian political system.

Judgement related to Council of Ministers

- In **S.R. Chauhan vs State of Punjab** (2001), Supreme Court held that a non-member cannot be re-appointed without being elected. However, a Non-member can also become a part of the council of ministers for a maximum of 6 months.
- The **oath by Devi Lal as Deputy Prime Minister in 1990 was challenged as being unconstitutional** as the Constitution provides only for the Prime Minister and other ministers.
- The Supreme Court upheld the oath as valid and stated that describing a person as Deputy PM is descriptive only and such description does not confer on him any powers of PM.
- SC ruled that the description of a minister as Deputy Prime Ministers or any other type of minister such as minister of state or deputy minister of which there is no mention in the Constitution does not vitiate the oath taken by him so long as the substantive part of the oath is correct.

Locksabha and Rajya Sabha

- **Rajya Sabha (The Council of States):**

  - **About:** It is the Upper House (Second Chamber or House of Elders) and it **represents the states and union territories** of the Indian Union.The Rajya Sabha is called the **permanent House of the Parliament** as it is never fully dissolved.
  - The **IV Schedule** of the Indian Constitution deals with the allocation of seats in the Rajya Sabha to the states and UTs.
  - **Composition:** The maximum strength of Rajya Sabha is **250** (out of which 238 members are representatives of the states & UTs (elected indirectly) and **12 are nominated by the President).Current strength of the house is 245,** 229 members represent the states, 4 members represent the UTs and 12 are nominated by the president.
  - **Election of Representatives:** The **representatives of states** are elected by the members of state legislative assemblies.
  - The **representatives of each UT** in the Rajya Sabha are indirectly elected by members of an electoral college specially constituted for the purpose. Only three UTs **(Delhi, Puducherry and Jammu & Kashmir)** have representation in Rajya Sabha (others don't have enough population).
  - The members nominated by the President are **those who have special knowledge or practical experience** in art, literature, science and social service.
  - The rationale is to provide eminent persons a place in the house without going through elections.
  - **Functions:** Rajya Sabha has an important role of **reviewing and altering the laws** initiated by the Lok Sabha.
  - It can also **initiate legislation** and a bill is required to pass through the Rajya Sabha in order to become a law.
  - **Power:**

    - **State Related Matters:** The Rajya Sabha provides representation to the States. Therefore, **any matter that affects the States must be referred to it** for its consent and approval.

      - If the Union Parliament wishes to remove/transfer a matter from the State list, the **approval of the Rajya Sabha is necessary.**

- **Lok Sabha (The House of the People):**

  - **About:** It is the **Lower House** (First Chamber or Popular House and it represents the people of India as a whole.
  - **Composition:** The maximum strength of the Lok Sabha is fixed at **550** out of which 530 members are to be the representatives of the states and 20 of the UTs.
  - The **current strength of Lok Sabha is 543**, out of which 530 members represent the states and 13 represent the UTs.
  - Earlier, the President also nominated two members from the Anglo-Indian community, but by the **95th Amendment Act, 2009,** this provision was valid till 2020 only.
  - **Election of Representatives:** The representatives of states are **directly elected by the people** from the territorial constituencies in the states.
  - By the **Union Territories (Direct Election to the House of the People) Act, 1965,** the members of Lok Sabha from the UTs are chosen by direct election.
  - **Functions:** One of the most important functions of the Lok Sabha is to **select the executive,** a group of persons who work together to implement the laws made by the Parliament.

    - This executive is often what we have in mind when we use the term government.

  - **Powers:**

    - **Decisions in Joint Sitting:** Any ordinary law needs to be passed by both the Houses.
    - However, in case of any difference between the two Houses, the final decision is taken by calling a joint session of both the Houses.
    - Due to a larger strength, the **view of the Lok Sabha is likely to prevail** in such a meeting.
    - **Power in Money Matters:** Lok Sabha exercises **more powers in money matters.** Once the Lok Sabha passes the budget of the government or any other money related law, the **Rajya Sabha cannot reject it.**

- The Rajya Sabha can only delay it by 14 days or suggest changes in it, however, the former **may or may not accept these changes.**
- **Power over Council of Ministers:** The Lok Sabha **controls the Council of Ministers.**
- If the majority of the Lok Sabha members say they have 'no confidence' in the Council of Ministers, all ministers including the Prime Minister, have to quit.
- The Rajya Sabha does not have this power.

CHAPTER SIX

State Government

Article 153-167 in part six of the constitution deals with the state executive, therefore the constitution provides for a separate federal government with a distinct administrative setup. A state government is a branch of government that is responsible for enacting and enforcing state laws. State governments are used by some modern nations, like the United States, Australia, and India, to administer local concerns. Typically, state governments are in charge of administering a state's or region's local demands and concerns.

Governor

The Constitution has assigned a dual role for the governor, he is a constitutional head of the state as well as representative of the centre (President).

- The Governor is the State's chief executive. But, like the President, he/she is only a ceremonial head of State (titular or constitutional head).
- Normally, each State has its own Governor, but the 7th Constitutional Amendment Act of 1956 made it easier to appoint the same individual to serve as Governor of two or more States.
- All the executive actions of the state governments are to be taken in his/her name.
- As an integral part of the state legislature he can summon, prorogue or dissolve the state legislative assembly.
- His/Her financial powers enable him/her to introduce an annual financial statement in the assembly.
- Possess constitutional discretion in various scenarios.

Chief Minister

Is regarded as the real executive authority in the state. Under article 164 of the constitution the appointment of chief minister is done by the governor.

- The Chief Minister's position in the state is comparable to that of the Prime Minister at the centre.
- The Governor appoints the Chief Minister, according to Article 164 of the Constitution.
- If no party has a clear majority, the governor may use situational discretion. He may appoint a leader as chief minister and then demonstrate his majority on the floor of the parliament.
- Directs, controls, coordinates the activities of the council of ministers.
- Acts as the principal channel of communication between council of ministers and the governor.
- Announces the government policies on the floor of the house
- Is the political head of services of the state

State Council of Ministers

Article 163 addresses the status of the council of ministers and Article 164 addresses the ministers' appointment, tenure, responsibility, qualifications, oath, and salaries and allowances.

- The real executive authority in a state's politico-administrative system is the council of ministers, which is led by the chief minister.
- The states' councils of ministers are formed and function in the same way as the Centre's council of ministers.
- The council of ministers headed by the chief minister advise the governor.
- Council of ministers is collectively responsible to the legislative assembly of the state
- Ministers hold office during the pleasure of the governor.

State Legislature

Article 168 to 212 in part six of the constitution deals with the organisation, powers, privileges, etc of the state legislature.

- **Legislative Assembly:** The Legislative Assembly is a legislature that is elected by the people and is the true seat of power in a state.
- An assembly's maximum strength must not exceed 500, and its minimum strength must not be less than 60.
- **Legislative Council:** The Legislative Council of a State is made up of not more than one-third of the members of the State's Legislative Assembly and in no case less than 40.

Special Provisions for some States

These special provisions were not incorporated in the original constitution, but were incorporated with subsequent amendments during reorganization of states.

- In 1969, the 5th Finance Commission introduced the concept of Special Category Status, recognizing that some sections of the country had historically been disadvantaged in comparison to others.
- **Aim:** To grant preferential treatment to disadvantaged states in the form of central support and tax cuts. The National Development Council has previously provided assistance to various states under the Central Plan.
- Initially, only three states were given special status: Assam, Nagaland, and Jammu and Kashmir.

Supreme Court And High Court

1. The present-day Supreme Court of India started functioning on January 28, 1950. Its predecessor was the Federal Court of India, which was created as per the Government of India Act of 1935.
2. Articles 124 to 147 mentioned in Part V of the Constitution deal with the organisation, independence, jurisdiction, powers, and procedures and so on of the Supreme Court.
3. At present, the strength of Supreme Court's judges stands at thirty-one judges (one chief justice and thirty-three other judges).

4. Originally, the strength of the Supreme Court was fixed at eight (one chief justice and seven other judges).

5. **Appointment**- The judges of the Supreme Court are appointed by the president. The appointment of the Chief Justice is made by the president after consultation with such judges of the Supreme Court and high courts as he deems necessary. The other judges are appointed by the president after consultation with the chief justice and such other judges of the Supreme Court and the high courts as he deems necessary. The consultation with the chief justice is obligatory in the case of appointment of a judge other than Chief justice.

6. In 2015 the National Judicial Appointments Commission was declared Ultra Vires by the Supreme Court and hence the collegium system still holds the ground mentioned above.

7. **Qualification**- A person to be appointed as a judge of the Supreme Court should have the following qualifications:
(i) He should be a citizen of India.
(ii) (a) He should have been a judge of a High Court (or high courts in succession) for five years, or (b) He should have been an advocate of a High Court (or High Courts in succession) for ten years; or (c) He should be a distinguished jurist in the opinion of the president.

1. **Oath**- The oath to the judges and CJI is administered by the President or any other person appointed by him for this purpose.

2. **Tenure of Judges** - A. He holds office until he attains the age of 65 years. B. He can resign his office by writing to the president. C. He can be removed from his office by the President on the recommendation of the Parliament.

3. **Removal of Judges** A judge of the Supreme Court can be removed from his office by an order of the President. However, he can do so only after an address by Parliament has been presented to him in the same session for such removal. The address must be supported by a *special majority* of each House of Parliament - a majority of the total membership of that House and a majority of not less than two-thirds of the members of that House present and voting. The grounds of removal are —proved misbehaviour or incapacity.

4. The removal process of both the Supreme Court and High courts are the same.

5. The jurisdiction and powers of the Supreme Court can be classified into-Original Jurisdiction, Writ Jurisdiction, Appellate Jurisdiction, Advisory Jurisdiction, A court of Record and so on.

6. Original Jurisdiction - when the case is involved between centre and states or two or more states or centre and two or more states being anti. The first such instance came in 1961 in West Bengal VS the centre.

7. The Constitution has constituted the Supreme Court as the guarantor and defender of the fundamental rights of the citizens. The Supreme Court is empowered to issue writs including *habeas corpus, mandamus,* prohibition, *quo-warranto* and *certiorari* for the enforcement of the fundamental rights of an aggrieved citizen. The difference between the supreme court's and high court's writ jurisdiction is that the supreme court can issue writs in cases involving only fundamental rights and the high courts can issue writs otherwise as well.

THE HIGH COURTS

1. The institution of high court originated in India in 1862 when the high courts were set up at Calcutta, Bombay and Madras. The fourth one was established at Allahabad in 1866 and subsequently in other provinces in British India and then as they were called states after independence.

2. As per the Seventh Amendment Act of 1956, the Parliament can establish a common high court for two or more States or for two or more states and a union territory.

3. At present, there are 24 high courts in the country. Out of them, three are common high courts. Delhi is the only union territory that has a high court of its own (since 1966). The other union territories fall under the jurisdiction of different state high courts.

4. **Appointment of Judges** The judges of a high court are appointed by the President. The chief justice of the High Court is appointed by the President after consultation with the chief justice of India and the governor of the state concerned. For the appointment of other judges, the chief justice of the concerned high court is also consulted. In case of a common high court for two or more states, the governors of all the states concerned are consulted by the president.

5. **Qualifications of Judges** A person to be appointed as a judge of a high court should have the following qualifications: A. He should be a citizen of India. B. (a) He should have held a judicial office in the territory of

India for ten years, or (b) He should have been an advocate of a high court (or high courts in succession) for ten years.

6. **Oath or Affirmation** Oath to the judge is administered by the governor of the state or some person appointed by him for this purpose.

7. **Tenure of Judges** - A. He holds office until he attains the age of 62 years. B. He can resign his office by writing to the president. C. He can be removed from his office by the President on the recommendation of the Parliament. D. He vacates his office when he is appointed as a judge of the Supreme Court or when he is transferred to another high court.

Judicial system of India

\The judiciary is that branch of the government that interprets the law, settles disputes and administers justice to all citizens. The judiciary is considered the watchdog of democracy, and also the guardian of the Constitution. For democracy to function effectively, it is imperative to have an impartial and independent judiciary.

Independent Indian Judiciary

- It means that the other branches of the government, namely, the executive and the legislature, does not interfere with the judiciary's functioning.
- The judiciary's decision is respected and not interfered with by the other organs.
- It also means that judges can perform their duties without fear or favour.

Independence of the judiciary also does not mean that the judiciary functions arbitrarily and without any accountability. It is accountable to the Constitution of the country.

Indian Judiciary – Structure

India has a single integrated judicial system. The judiciary in India has a pyramidal structure with the Supreme Court (SC) at the top. High Courts are below the SC, and below them are the district and subordinate courts. The lower courts function under the direct superintendence of the higher courts.

Apart from the above structure, there are also **two branches of the legal system**, which are:

1. **Criminal Law:** These deal with the committing of a crime by any citizen/entity. A criminal case starts when the local police file a crime report. The court finally decides on the matter.
2. **Civil Law:** These deal with disputes over the violation of the Fundamental Rights of a citizen.

Supreme Court has three types of jurisdictions. They are original, appellate and advisory. The jurisdiction of the Supreme Court is mentioned in Articles 131, 133, 136 and 143 of the Constitution.

Functions of Indian Judiciary – What is the role of the Judiciary?

The functions of the judiciary in India are:

1. **Administration of justice:** The chief function of the judiciary is to apply the law to specific cases or in settling disputes. When a dispute is brought before the courts it 'determines the facts' involved through evidence presented by the contestants. The law then proceeds to decide what law is applicable to the case and applies it. If someone is found guilty of violating the law in the course of the trial, the court will impose a penalty on the guilty person.
2. **Creation of judge-case law:** In many cases, the judges are not able to, or find it difficult to select the appropriate law for application. In such cases, the judges decide what the appropriate law is on the basis of their wisdom and common sense. In doing so, judges have built up a great body of 'judge-made law' or 'case law.' As per the doctrine of 'stare decisis', the previous decisions of judges are generally regarded as binding on later judges in similar cases.
3. **Guardian of the Constitution:** The highest court in India, the SC, acts as the guardian of the Constitution. The conflicts of jurisdiction between the central government and the state governments or between the legislature and the executive are decided by the court. Any law or executive order which violates any provision of the constitution is declared unconstitutional or null and void by the judiciary. This is called

'judicial review.' Judicial review has the merit of guaranteeing the fundamental rights of individuals and ensuring a balance between the union and the units in a federal state.

4. **Protector of Fundamental Rights:** The judiciary ensures that people's rights are not trampled upon by the State or any other agency. The superior courts enforce Fundamental Rights by issuing writs.

5. **Supervisory functions:** The higher courts also perform the function of supervising the subordinate courts in India.

6. **Advisory functions:** The SC in India performs an advisory function as well. It can give its advisory opinions on constitutional questions. This is done in the absence of disputes and when the executive so desires.

7. **Administrative functions:** Some functions of the courts are non-judicial or administrative in nature. The courts may grant certain licenses, administer the estates (property) of deceased persons and appoint receivers. They register marriages, appoint guardians of minor children and lunatics.

8. **Special role in a federation:** In a federal system like India's, the judiciary also performs the important task of settling disputes between the centre and states. It also acts as an arbiter of disputes between states.

9. **Conducting judicial enquiries:** Judges normally are called to head commissions that enquire into cases of errors or omissions on the part of public servants.

Indian Judiciary – Civil Courts

Civil courts deal with civil cases. Civil law is referred to in almost all cases other than criminal cases. Criminal law applies when a crime such as a robbery, murder, arson, etc. is perpetrated.

- Civil law is applied in disputes when one person sues another person or entity. Examples of civil cases include divorce, eviction, consumer problems, debt or bankruptcy, etc.
- Judges in civil courts and criminal courts have different powers. While a judge in a criminal court can punish the convicted person by sending him/her to jail, a judge in a civil court can make the guilty pay fines, etc.
- District Judges sitting in District Courts and Magistrates of Second Class and Civil Judge (Junior Division) are at the bottom of the judicial

hierarchy in India.

- The court of the district judges is the highest civil court in a district.
- It has both administrative and judicial powers.
- The court of the District Judge is in the district HQ.
- It can try criminal and civil cases and hence, the judge is called District and Sessions Judge.
- Under the district courts, there are courts of the Sub-Judge, Additional Sub-Judge and Munsif Courts.
- Most civil cases are filed in the Munsif's court.

Civil courts have four types of jurisdiction:

- **Subject Matter Jurisdiction:** It can try cases of a particular type and relate to a particular subject.
- **Territorial Jurisdiction:** It can try cases within its geographical limit, and not beyond the territory.
- **Pecuniary Jurisdiction:** Cases related to money matters, suits of monetary value.
- **Appellate Jurisdiction:** This is the authority of a court to hear appeals or review a case that has already been decided by a lower court. The Supreme Court and the High Courts have appellate jurisdiction to hear cases that were decided by a lower court

CHAPTER SEVEN

Local Self Government

- Local Self Government is the management of local affairs by such local bodies who have been elected by the local people.
- The local self-Government includes **both rural and urban government.**
- It is the **third level of the government.**
- There are **2 types of local government in operation** – panchayatas in rural areas and Municipalities in urban areas.

- **Rural Local Governments:**

  - Panchayati Raj Institution (PRI) is a system of rural local self-government in India.
  - PRI was constitutionalized through the **73rd Constitutional Amendment** Act, 1992 to build democracy at the grass roots level and was entrusted with the task of rural development in the country.

    - This act has added a new Part-IX to the Constitution of India. This part is entitled as 'The Panchayats' and consists of provisions from **Articles 243 to 243 O.**
    - In addition, the act has also added a new Eleventh Schedule to the Constitution. This schedule contains 29 functional items of the panchayats. It deals with Article 243-G.

  - In its present form and structure PRI has completed 30 years of existence. However, a lot remains to be done in order to further decentralization and strengthen democracy at the grass root level.

- **Urban Local Governments:**

  - <u>Urban Local Governments</u> were established with the purpose of democratic decentralisation.
  - There are **eight types of urban local governments in India** - Municipal Corporation, Municipality, Notified Area Committee, Town Area Committee, Cantonment Board, township, port trust, special purpose agency.
  - At the Central level the subject of 'urban local government' is dealt with by the following three Ministries.

    - The Ministry of Urban Development was created as a separate ministry in 1985 (now Ministry of Housing and Urban Affairs).
    - Ministry of Defense in the case of cantonment boards.
    - Ministry of Home Affairs in the case of Union Territories.

  - The 74th Amendment Act pertaining to urban local government was passed during the regime of P.V. Narsimha Rao's government in 1992. It came into force on 1st June, 1993.

    - Added Part IX -A and consists of provisions from articles 243-P to 243-ZG.
    - Added 12th Schedule to the Constitution. It contains 18 functional items of Municipalities and deals with Article 243 W.

What are the Salient Features of 73rd Constitutional Amendment?

- **Compulsory Provisions:**

  - Organisation of Gram Sabhas;
  - Creation of a three-tier Panchayati Raj Structure at the Zila, Block and Village levels;
  - Almost all posts, at all levels to be filled by direct elections;
  - Minimum age for contesting elections to the Panchayati Raj institutions be twenty one years;

- The post of Chairman at the Zila and Block levels should be filled by indirect election;
- There should be reservation of seats for Scheduled Castes/ Scheduled Tribes in Panchayats, in proportion to their population, and for women in Panchayats up to one-third seats;
- State Election Commission to be set up in each State to conduct elections to Panchayati Raj institutions;
- The tenure of Panchayati Raj institutions is five years, if dissolved earlier, fresh elections to be held within six months;
- A State Finance Commission is set up in each State every five years.

- **Voluntary:**

  - Giving voting rights to members of the Central and State legislatures in these bodies;
  - Providing reservation for backward classes; and
  - The Panchayati Raj institutions should be given financial powers in relation to taxes, levy fees etc. and efforts shall be made to make Panchayats autonomous bodies.

What are the Salient Features of 74th Amendment Act?

- **Compulsory:**

  - Constitution of nagar panchayats, municipal councils and municipal corporations in small, big and very big urban areas respectively;
  - Reservation of seats in urban local bodies for Scheduled Castes / Scheduled Tribes roughly in proportion to their population;
  - Reservation of seats for women up to one-third seats;
  - The State Election Commission, constituted in order to conduct elections in the Panchayati raj bodies (see 73rd Amendment) will also conduct elections to the urban local self- governing bodies;
  - The State Finance Commission, constituted to deal with financial affairs of the panchayati raj bodies also looks into the financial affairs of the local urban selfgoverning bodies;

- ◦ Tenure of urban local self-governing bodies is fixed at five years and in case of earlier dissolution fresh elections are held within six months;

- **Voluntary:**

  - ◦ Giving voting rights to members of the Union and State Legislatures in these bodies;
  - ◦ Providing reservation for backward classes;
  - ◦ Giving financial powers in relation to taxes, duties, tolls and fees, etc;
  - ◦ Making the municipal bodies autonomous and devolution of powers to these bodies to perform some or all of the functions enumerated in the Twelfth Schedule added to the Constitution through this Act and/or to prepare plans for economic development.

Introduction to Panchayati Raj

Rural development is one of the main objectives of Panchayati Raj and this has been established in all states of India except Nagaland, Meghalaya and Mizoram, in all Union Territories except Delhi. and certain other areas. These areas include:

a. The scheduled areas and the tribal areas in the states
b. The hill area of Manipur for which a district council exists and
c. Darjeeling district of West Bengal for which Darjeeling Gorkha Hill Council exists

Evolution of Panchayati Raj

The Panchayati system in India is not purely a post-independence phenomenon. In fact, the dominant political institution in rural India has been the village panchayat for centuries. In ancient India, panchayats were usually elected councils with executive and judicial powers. Foreign domination, especially Mughal and British, and the natural and forced socio-economic changes had undermined the importance of the village panchayats. In the pre-independence period, however, the panchayats were instruments for the dominance of the upper castes over the rest of the village, which furthered the divide based on either the socio-economic status or the caste hierarchy.

The evolution of the Panchayati Raj System, however, got a fillip after the attainment of independence after the drafting of the Constitution. The Constitution of India in Article 40 enjoined: "The state shall take steps to organise village panchayats and endow them with such powers and authority as may be necessary to enable them to function as units of self-government".

There were a number of committees appointed by the Government of India to study the implementation of self-government at the rural level and also recommend steps in achieving this goal.

The committees appointed are as follows:

- Balwant Rai Mehta Committee
- Ashok Mehta Committee
- G V K Rao Committee
- L M Singhvi Committee

Balwant Rai Mehta Committee & Panchayati Raj

The committee was appointed in 1957, to examine and suggest measures for better working of the Community Development Programme and the National Extension Service. The committee suggested the establishment of a democratic decentralised local government which came to be known as the Panchayati Raj.

Recommendations by the Committee:

- Three-tier Panchayati Raj system: Gram Panchayat, Panchayat Samiti and Zila Parishad.
- Directly elected representatives to constitute the gram panchayat and indirectly elected representatives to constitute the Panchayat Samiti and Zila Parishad.
- Planning and development are the primary objectives of the Panchayati Raj system.
- Panchayat Samiti should be the executive body and Zila Parishad will act as the advisory and supervisory body.

- District Collector to be made the chairman of the Zila Parishad.
- It also requested for provisioning resources so as to help them discharge their duties and responsibilities.

The Balwant Rai Mehta Committee further revitalised the development of panchayats in the country, the report recommended that the Panchayati Raj institutions can play a substantial role in community development programmes throughout the country. The objective of the Panchayats thus was the democratic decentralisation through the effective participation of locals with the help of well-planned programmes. Even the then Prime Minister of India, Pandit Jawaharlal Nehru, defended the panchayat system by saying, authority and power must be given to the people in the villages Let us give power to the panchayats."

Ashok Mehta Committee & Panchayati Raj

The committee was appointed in 1977 to suggest measures to revive and strengthen the declining Panchayati Raj system in India.
The key recommendations are:

- The three-tier system should be replaced with a two-tier system: Zila Parishad (district level) and the Mandal Panchayat (a group of villages).
- District level as the first level of supervision after the state level.
- Zila Parishad should be the executive body and responsible for planning at the district level.
- The institutions (Zila Parishad and the Mandal Panchayat) to have compulsory taxation powers to mobilise their own financial resources.

G V K Rao Committee & Panchayati Raj

The committee was appointed by the planning commission in 1985. It recognised that development was not seen at the grassroot level due to bureaucratisation resulting in Panchayat Raj institutions being addressed as 'grass without roots'. Hence, it made some key recommendations which are as follows:

- Zila Parishad to be the most important body in the scheme of democratic decentralisation. Zila Parishad to be the principal body to manage the developmental programmes at the district level.
- The district and the lower levels of the Panchayati Raj system to be assigned with specific planning, implementation and monitoring of the rural developmental programmes.
- Post of District Development Commissioner to be created. He will be the chief executive officer of the Zila Parishad.
- Elections to the levels of Panchayati Raj systems should be held regularly.

L M Singhvi Committee & Panchayati Raj

The committee was appointed by the Government of India in 1986 with the main objective to recommend steps to revitalise the Panchayati Raj systems for democracy and development. The following recommendations were made by the committee:

- The committee recommended that the Panchayati Raj systems should be constitutionally recognised. It also recommended constitutional provisions to recognise free and fair elections for the Panchayati Raj systems.
- The committee recommended reorganisation of villages to make the gram panchayat more viable.
- It recommended that village panchayats should have more finances for their activities.
- Judicial tribunals to be set up in each state to adjudicate matters relating to the elections to the Panchayati Raj institutions and other matters relating to their functioning.

All these things further the argument that panchayats can be very effective in identifying and solving local problems, involve the people in the villages in the developmental activities, improve the communication between different levels at which politics operates, develop leadership skills and in short help the basic development in the states without making too many structural changes. Rajasthan and Andhra Pradesh were the first to adopt Panchayati raj in 1959, other states followed them later.

Though there are variations among states, there are some features that are common. In most of the states, for example, a three-tier structure including panchayats at the village level, panchayat samitis at the block level and the zila parishads at the district level-has been institutionalized. Due to the sustained effort of the civil society organisations, intellectuals and progressive political leaders, the Parliament passed two amendments to the Constitution – the 73rd Constitution Amendment for rural local bodies (panchayats) and the 74th Constitution Amendment for urban local bodies (municipalities) making them 'institutions of self-government'. Within a year all the states passed their own acts in conformity to the amended constitutional provisions.

73rd *Constitutional Amendment Act of 1992*

Significance of the Act

- The Act added Part IX to the Constitution, "The Panchayats" and also added the Eleventh Schedule which consists of the 29 functional items of the panchayats.
- Part IX of the Constitution contains Article 243 to Article 243 O.
- The Amendment Act provides shape to Article 40 of the Constitution, (directive principles of state policy), which directs the state to organise the village panchayats and provide them powers and authority so that they can function as self-government.
- With the Act, Panchayati Raj systems come under the purview of the justiciable part of the Constitution and mandates states to adopt the system. Further, the election process in the Panchayati Raj institutions will be held independent of the state government's will.
- The Act has two parts: compulsory and voluntary. Compulsory provisions must be added to state laws, which includes the creation of the new Panchayati Raj systems. Voluntary provisions, on the other hand, is the discretion of the state government.
- The Act is a very significant step in creating democratic institutions at the grassroots level in the country. The Act has transformed the representative democracy into participatory democracy.

Salient Features of the Act

1. Gram Sabha: Gram Sabha is the primary body of the Panchayati Raj system. It is a village assembly consisting of all the registered voters within the area of the panchayat. It will exercise powers and perform such functions as determined by the state legislature. Candidates can refer to the functions of gram panchayat and gram panchayat work, on the government official website – https://grammanchitra.gov.in/.

2. Three-tier system: The Act provides for the establishment of the three-tier system of Panchayati Raj in the states (village, intermediate and district level). States with a population of less than 20 lakhs may not constitute the intermediate level.

3. Election of members and chairperson: The members to all the levels of the Panchayati Raj are elected directly and the chairpersons to the intermediate and the district level are elected indirectly from the elected members and at the village level the Chairperson is elected as determined by the state government.

4. Reservation of seats:

   - For SC and ST: Reservation to be provided at all the three tiers in accordance with their population percentage.
   - For women: Not less than one-third of the total number of seats to be reserved for women, further not less than one-third of the total number of offices for chairperson at all levels of the panchayat to be reserved for women.
   - The state legislatures are also given the provision to decide on the reservation of seats in any level of panchayat or office of chairperson in favour of backward classes.

5. Duration of Panchayat: The Act provides for a five-year term of office to all the levels of the panchayat. However, the panchayat can be dissolved before the completion of its term. But fresh elections to constitute the new panchayat shall be completed –

   - before the expiry of its five-year duration.
   - in case of dissolution, before the expiry of a period of six months from the date of its dissolution.

6. Disqualification: A person shall be disqualified for being chosen as or for being a member of panchayat if he is so disqualified –

- Under any law for the time being in force for the purpose of elections to the legislature of the state concerned.
- Under any law made by the state legislature. However, no person shall be disqualified on the ground that he is less than 25 years of age if he has attained the age of 21 years.
- Further, all questions relating to disqualification shall be referred to an authority determined by the state legislatures.

7. State election commission:

- The commission is responsible for superintendence, direction and control of the preparation of electoral rolls and conducting elections for the panchayat.
- The state legislature may make provisions with respect to all matters relating to elections to the panchayats.

1. Powers and Functions: The state legislature may endow the Panchayats with such powers and authority as may be necessary to enable them to function as institutions of self-government. Such a scheme may contain provisions related to Gram Panchayat work with respect to:

- the preparation of plans for economic development and social justice.
- the implementation of schemes for economic development and social justice as may be entrusted to them, including those in relation to the 29 matters listed in the Eleventh Schedule.

2. Finances: The state legislature may –

- Authorize a panchayat to levy, collect and appropriate taxes, duties, tolls and fees.
- Assign to a panchayat taxes, duties, tolls and fees levied and collected by the state government.
- Provide for making grants-in-aid to the panchayats from the consolidated fund of the state.
- Provide for the constitution of funds for crediting all money of the panchayats.

10. Finance Commission: The state finance commission reviews the financial position of the panchayats and provides recommendations for the necessary steps to be taken to supplement resources to the panchayat.

11. Audit of Accounts: State legislature may make provisions for the maintenance and audit of panchayat accounts.

12. Application to Union Territories: The President may direct the provisions of the Act to be applied on any union territory subject to exceptions and modifications he specifies.

13. Exempted states and areas: The Act does not apply to the states of Nagaland, Meghalaya and Mizoram and certain other areas. These areas include,

   - The scheduled areas and the tribal areas in the states
   - The hill area of Manipur for which a district council exists
   - Darjeeling district of West Bengal for which Darjeeling Gorkha Hill Council exists.
     However, Parliament can extend this part to these areas subject to the exception and modification it specifies. Thus, the PESA Act was enacted.

14. Continuance of existing law: All the state laws relating to panchayats shall continue to be in force until the expiry of one year from the commencement of this Act. In other words, the states have to adopt the new Panchayati raj system based on this Act within the maximum period of one year from 24 April 1993, which was the date of the commencement of this Act. However, all the Panchayats existing immediately before the commencement of the Act shall continue till the expiry of their term, unless dissolved by the state legislature sooner.

15. Bar to interference by courts: The Act bars the courts from interfering in the electoral matters of panchayats. It declares that the validity of any law relating to the delimitation of constituencies or the allotment of seats to such constituencies cannot be questioned in any court. It further lays down that no election to any panchayat is to be questioned except by an election petition presented to such authority and in such manner as provided by the state legislature.

PESA Act of 1996

The provisions of Part IX are not applicable to the Fifth Schedule areas. The Parliament can extend this Part to such areas with modifications and exceptions as it may specify. Under these provisions, Parliament enacted Provisions of the Panchayats (Extension to the Scheduled Areas) Act, popularly known as PESA Act or the extension act.

Objectives of the PESA Act:

1. To extend the provisions of Part IX to the scheduled areas.
2. To provide self-rule for the tribal population.
3. To have village governance with participatory democracy.
4. To evolve participatory governance consistent with the traditional practices.
5. To preserve and safeguard traditions and customs of tribal population.
6. To empower panchayats with powers conducive to tribal requirements.
7. To prevent panchayats at a higher level from assuming powers and authority of panchayats at a lower level.

As a result of these constitutional steps taken by the union and state governments, India has moved towards what has been described as 'multi-level federalism', and more significantly, it has widened the democratic base of the Indian polity. Before the amendments, the Indian democratic structure through elected representatives was restricted to the two houses of Parliament, state assemblies and certain union territories. The system has brought governance and issue redressal to the grassroot levels in the country but there are other issues too. These issues, if addressed, will go a long way in creating an environment where some of the basic human rights are respected.

After the new generation of panchayats had started functioning, several issues have come to the fore, which have a bearing on human rights. The important factor which has contributed to the human rights situation vis-a-vis the panchayat system is the nature of Indian society, which of course determines the nature of the state. Indian society is known for its inequality, social hierarchy and the rich and poor divide. The social hierarchy is the result of the caste system, which is unique to India. Therefore, caste and class are the two factors, which deserve attention in this context.

Thus, the local governance system has challenged the age old practices of hierarchy in the rural areas of the country particularly those related to caste, religion and discrimination against women.

Central And State Govt Bodies

1. ATTORNEY GENERAL OF INDIA

- Article 76 of the Constitution provides for the Attorney General of India.
- He is considered the highest law officer in the country.
- He is appointed by the president and holds office during his pleasure.
- A person who is qualified to be appointed as the judge of the Supreme Court is eligible for the office of Attorney General of India.

Duties of AG:

- To advise the government on the legal matters referred to him by the president.
- To appear on behalf of the GOI in SC in all the cases concerning the government.
- To represent GOI in the references made by the president to the SC under Article 143.
- To appear in HC in the cases concerning GOI when required.

Rights of AG:

- AG has the right to audience in all the courts in the territory of India.
- He has the right to speak and take part in the parliamentary proceedings. However, he doesn't enjoy the right to vote.
- All the privileges and immunities available to a member of parliament are granted to the AG.

2. COMPTROLLER AND AUDITOR GENERAL OF INDIA

- Article 148 of the Constitution provides for an independent office of Comptroller and Auditor General of India.

- CAG is considered as the guardian of the public purse.
- Along with the Supreme Court, the Election Commission, and the Union Public Service Commission, the office of CAG is treated as one of the bulwarks of the democratic system.

Appointment:

- President of India appoints CAG by a warrant under his hand and seal.
- He holds office for a period of six years or up to the age of 65 years, whichever is earlier.
- CAG can be removed from his office in the same manner as a judge of the Supreme Court.

Independence:

- CAG is provided with the security of tenure.
- His rights cannot be altered to his disadvantage after his appointment.
- All the expenses of the office of CAG are charged on the Consolidated Fund of India.
- His salary is equal to that of a judge of the Supreme Court.

Duties:

- The duties and powers of CAG are mentioned in article 149 of the Constitution.
- All the accounts related to the expenses from the Consolidated Fund of India, Consolidated Fund of the States, and Union Territories are audited by CAG.
- Also, the expenditure from Contingency Fund and Public Account of India and States are audited by CAG.
- The net proceeds of any tax or duty are ascertained and certified by CAG.
- CAG acts as a guide, friend, and philosopher of the Public Accounts Committee.
- All the receipts and expenditure of bodies financed from the central or state revenue are also audited by CAG.
- The audits of any other body as and when requested by the President or Governor are audited by CAG.

- Three reports are submitted by CAG to the President. They are: (1) Audit report on appropriation accounts (2) Audit report on finance accounts (3) Audit report on public undertakings

Role of CAG:

- The office of CAG secures the accountability of the executive to the Parliament in the sphere of financial administration.
- The CAG acts as an agent of the Parliament and is responsible only to the Parliament.
- Along with legal and regulatory audits, CAG also conducts propriety audits.

3. ADVOCATE GENERAL OF THE STATE

- Article 165 of the Constitution provides for <u>Advocate General for the states</u>.
- He is considered the highest law officer in the state.
- The Advocate General is appointed by the governor and holds the office during his pleasure.
- A person qualified to be appointed as a judge of a high court is eligible for the office of Advocate General.

Duties and Rights of Advocate General:

- To advise the government of the state on the matters referred to him by the governor.
- To discharge those functions conferred upon him by the Constitution of India.
- He has the right to speak and take part in the proceedings of both the houses of the state legislature. However, he doesn't enjoy the right to vote.

4. STATE FINANCE COMMISSION

- The governor of a state shall, after every five years, constitute a finance commission.
- Articles 243-I and 243-Y deal with the formation of this body.
- The composition, qualifications of members, and the manner of their selection is decided by the concerned state legislature.

Functions:

- The distribution of the net proceeds of taxes, tolls, and fees between the state and local bodies.
- The determination of such taxes, duties, and tolls to be assigned to local bodies.
- The grants-in-aid to be given to the local bodies from the consolidated fund of the state.
- Measures to be taken for improving the financial position of local bodies.
- Any other matter referred to the commission by the governor of the state.

5. STATE ELECTION COMMISSION

- The elections to the panchayats and municipalities are looked after by the State Election Commission.
- Articles 243-K and 243-ZA deal with the elections to the rural and urban local bodies.
- SEC consists of a state election commissioner who is appointed by the governor.
- The removal of the state election commissioner is the same as that of a judge of the state high court.

6. DISTRICT PLANNING COMMITTEE

- A district planning committee is constituted and given the task to consolidate the plans of both panchayats and municipalities.
- It prepares a draft development plan for the district.

- Article 243-ZD deals with the committee for district planning.
- The composition, manner of election of chairperson and members is decided by the state legislature.
- Four-fifths of the committee are elected by the elected members of panchayats and municipalities.
- The representation of these members is proportional to the ratio of the rural and urban population in the district.
- In preparing the plan, DPC should consider the following:

1. Matters of common interest between the rural and urban local bodies regarding sharing of resources, infrastructure development, and conservation of environment.
2. Extent and type of resources available.

7. *METROPOLITAN PLANNING COMMITTEE*

- A metropolitan planning committee is constituted for every metropolitan area.
- Article 243 -ZE deals with the committee for metropolitan planning.
- The composition, manner of election of chairpersons and members, functions, etc are decided by the concerned state legislature.
- Two-thirds of MPC are elected by the elected members of the municipalities and chairpersons of panchayats.
- The representation of these members is proportional to the ratio of the population of municipalities and panchayats.
- While preparing the draft plan, the committee shall consider:

1. Plans of municipalities and panchayats in the metropolitan area.
2. Matters of common interest between the rural and urban local bodies regarding sharing of resources, infrastructural development and conservation of environment.
3. The extent of investments to be made in the concerned metropolitan area.
4. Objectives and priorities of the center and the concerned state.

8. INTER-STATE COUNCIL

- Article 263 deals with the establishment of <u>Inter-State Councils</u> for the coordination between centre and states as well among the different states.
- The president establishes such a council and also defines its duties and organization.
- Its decision is advisory in nature and is not binding.

Composition:

- The council consists of the following members:

1. Prime Minister as the chairman
2. Chief Ministers of all the states and union territories having a legislative assembly
3. Administrators of union territories with no legislative assemblies
4. Governors of states under the president's rule
5. Six central cabinet ministers nominated by PM

- The council consists of a standing committee set up in 1996. Its members are:

1. Union Home Minister as the chairman
2. Five Union Cabinet Ministers
3. Nine Chief Ministers

9. FINANCE COMMISSION

- <u>Finance Commission</u> is a quasi-judicial body.
- The formation of FC is provided by the constitution under article 280.
- It is constituted every fifth year or at such an earlier time as the president of India considers necessary.

Composition:

- FC consists of a chairman and four other members appointed by the president.
- The qualification of the members and the manner of their selection is determined by parliament.
- They are eligible for reappointment.
- The four members should be selected from amongst the following:

1. A judge of HC or one qualified to be appointed as such.
2. A person with specialized knowledge in finance and accounts of the government.
3. A person with wide experience in financial matters and administration.
4. A person with special knowledge in economics.

Functions:

- FC makes recommendations to the president on the following matters:

1. Distribution and allocation of the net proceeds of the taxes between center and states and also among different states.
2. The principles that should govern the grants-in-aid to the states.
3. Measures needed to augment the consolidated fund of the state to supplement the resources of local bodies.
4. Any other matter referred to it by the president of India.

Role of FC:

- The commission submits its report to the president who lays it before both the Houses of the Parliament.
- The recommendations made by FC are only advisory in nature and are not binding on the government.
- Finance Commission is envisaged as the balancing wheel of fiscal federalism in India.

10. GOODS AND SERVICES TAX COUNCIL

- GST council is formed under article 279-A.

- Its function is to make recommendations to center and state governments regarding GST.
- It has representation from both centre and states and hence is a federal body.
- GST council consists of the following members:

1. Union Finance Minister as Chairperson

   Union Minister of State in charge of revenue or finance as a membe

1. Minister in charge of revenue or finance or any other minister nominated by the state government as members.

- The decisions of the council are taken by a majority of not less than three-fourths of weighted votes cast by the members present and voting.
- The weightage of the vote of the central government is one-third of the total votes and the weightage of votes of state government is two-thirds of all votes cast.
- It aims to uphold the principle of cooperative federalism.

11. UNION PUBLIC SERVICE COMMISSION

- UPSC is the central recruiting agency of the country.
- Articles 315 to 323 in Part XIV of the constitution talk about UPSC.
- UPSC is visualized as the watchdog of the merit system of the country.

Composition:

- UPSC consists of a chairman and other members. The number of other members is left to the discretion of the president.
- Generally, the number of members in the commission including the chairman is nine to eleven.
- They hold the office for a term of six years or until they attain the age of 65 years, whichever is earlier.

Removal:

- The chairman and other members of UPSC can be removed by the president under the following situations:

1. If he is adjudged an insolvent
2. While in office, if he engages in any paid employment
3. If he gets unfit by reason of infirmity of mind or body
4. For misbehavior

- In the last case, the president has to refer the matter to Supreme Court for inquiry. The advice of SC is binding on the president.

Independence:

- The chairman and the members of the commission enjoy the security of tenure.
- Their conditions of service cannot be varied after an appointment.
- Their entire expenses are charged on the Consolidated Fund of India.
- The chairman of UPSC is not eligible for any future employment in the government of India or a state.

Functions:

- Examinations for recruitment to All India Services, central services, and public services of union territories are held by UPSC.
- All disciplinary matters affecting a person in civil capacity are dealt with by UPSC.
- Assists the states in matters relating to joint recruitment.

12. STATE PUBLIC SERVICE COMMISSION

- Just as UPSC at the center, there is a State Public Service Commission in every state.
- Articles 315 to 323 in part XIV of the constitution deal with the various provisions of SPSC.
- SPSC is considered as the watchdog of the merit system in the state.

Composition:

- SPSC consists of a chairman and other members appointed by the governor. The number of other members is left to the discretion of the governor.
- One-half of the members should be such persons who have held office either under the government of India or the state for at least ten years.
- The term of office is six years or until they attain the age of 62 years, whichever is earlier.

Removal:

- The chairman and members of the commission can be removed only by the president.
- They can be removed under the following situations:

1. If he is adjudged an insolvent
2. If he engages in any other paid employment
3. If he is deemed unfit by reason of infirmity of body or mind
4. For misbehavior

- In the last case, the president has to refer the matter to SC for inquiry.

Independence:

- The chairman and the members of the commission enjoy the security of tenure.
- Their conditions of service cannot be varied after an appointment.
- Their entire expenses are charged on the Consolidated Fund of the state.
- The chairman of SPSC is not eligible for any other employment under the government of India or state other than for appointment as chairman/ member of UPSC or as the chairman of other SPSC.

Functions:

- SPSC conducts all the examinations for the appointment to the services of the state.

- All disciplinary matters affecting a person in civil capacity are dealt with by SPSC.
- Any claim for reimbursement of legal expenses borne by a civil servant is also looked into by SPSC.

13. ELECTION COMMISSION

- Election Commission is a permanent and independent body.
- The formation of EC is prescribed by article 324 of the constitution.
- It is common to both central and state governments.
- The elections to parliament, state legislatures, the office of president, and vice president are looked after by EC.

Composition:

- EC consists of a chief election commissioner and other election commissioners. President fixes the number of election commissioners.
- The appointment of the chief election commissioner as well as the other election commissioners is made by the president.
- At present, EC consists of a chief election commissioner and two election commissioners.
- The term of office of election commissioners is six years or until they attain the age of 65 years, whichever is earlier.
- The powers of the election commission can be divided into three categories. They are:

1. Administrative
2. Advisory
3. Quasi-Judicial

Independence:

- Security of tenure is provided for the chief election commissioner.
- He can be removed from the office in the same manner as a judge of the Supreme Court.

- Other election commissioners cannot be removed from the office except on the recommendations of CEC.

14. NATIONAL COMMISSION FOR SCs

- It is established by article 338 of the constitution.
- Initially, there used to be a single commission for SCs and STs. However, the 89th Constitutional Amendment Act of 2003 bifurcated it into two separate bodies.
- Thus, a separate National Commission for SCs came into existence in 2004.

Composition:

- It consists of a chairperson, a vice-chairperson, and three other members.
- They are appointed by the President by warrant under his hand and scal.
- President determines their tenure as well as conditions of service.

Functions:

- The following are the functions of the commission:

1. To investigate the matters regarding various safeguards provided for SCs.
2. To inquire into the complaints related to the deprivation of the rights of SCs.
3. To advise on the planning process for the socio-economic development of SCs.
4. To submit reports to the president regarding the working of various safeguards.
5. To make recommendations to union and state governments regarding the measures to be taken for effective implementation of safeguards.
6. To discharge such other functions as the President may specify.

- On all the major policy matters regarding the welfare of SCs, the commission is consulted by the government.

15. NATIONAL COMMISSION FOR STs

- It is established by article 338-A of the constitution.
- The 89th Constitutional Amendment Act of 2003 inserted a new article 338-A.
- Thus, a separate commission for STs came into existence in 2004.

Composition:

- It consists of a chairperson, a vice-chairperson, and three other members.
- They are appointed by the president by warrant under his hand and seal.
- Their tenure and conditions of service are determined by the president.

Functions:

- The following are the functions of the commission:

1. To investigate the matters regarding various safeguards provided for STs.
2. To inquire into the complaints related to the deprivation of the rights of STs.
3. To advise on the planning process for the socio-economic development of STs.
4. To submit reports to the president regarding the working of various safeguards.

- On all the major policy matters regarding the welfare of STs, the commission is consulted by the government.

16. NATIONAL COMMISSION FOR BACKWARD CLASSES

- The 102nd Constitutional Amendment Act of 2018 made NCBC a constitutional body.

- This act inserted a new article 338-B into the constitution.
- Initially, NCBC was a statutory body formed through the National Commission for Backward Classes Act, 1993.

Structure:

- It consists of a Chairperson, Vice-Chairperson, and three other members.
- They are appointed by the president by warrant under his hand and seal.
- Their tenure and conditions of service are determined by the president.

Functions:

- The following are the functions of the commission:

1. To investigate the matters regarding various safeguards provided for socially and educationally backward classes.
2. To inquire into the complaints related to the deprivation of the rights of socially and educationally backward classes.
3. To advise on the planning process for the socio-economic development of socially and educationally backward classes.
4. To submit reports to the president regarding the working of various safeguards.

- NCBC is the competent authority to look into the grievances of backward classes.

17. SCHEDULED AREA AND SCHEDULED TRIBES COMMISSION

- To submit a report on the administration of schedule areas and welfare of the scheduled tribes, the president may appoint a commission.
- President defines the powers, composition, and procedure of the commission.
- The union government shall give directions to states to take measures for the welfare of the scheduled tribes.

18. BACKWARD CLASSES COMMISSION

- Under article 340 of the constitution, the government has the obligation to promote the welfare of OBCs.
- OBCs is a term used to define the socially and educationally backward sections of society.
- The first backward classes commission under the chairmanship of Kaka Kalelkar was established in 1953.
- This commission recommended the reservation for backward classes in government services and local bodies.
- However, the report was not accepted by the government.
- The second backward classes commission known as the Mandal Commission was established in 1979.

Mandal Commission Report:

- The commission submitted its report in 1980.
- It identified as many as 3743 castes to be socially and educationally backward.
- Excluding the Scheduled Castes and Scheduled Tribes, these castes constituted about 52% of the population.
- The commission proposed for 27 percent reservation for OBCs in government jobs so that the total reservation for SCs, STs and OBCs do not exceed 50 percent.

19. OFFICIAL LANGUAGE COMMISSION

- At the expiration of five years from the commencement of constitution and thereafter at the expiration of ten years from such commencement, the president shall appoint such a commission.
- The commission recommends the president regarding the progressive use of Hindi for official purposes.
- It also recommends restrictions on the usage of the English language for official purposes.

- Also, the Official Language Act (1963) provided for setting up a Committee on Official Language.
- Its purpose was to review the progress made in the use of Hindi.
- Such a committee was set up in 1976.

20. SPECIAL OFFICER FOR LINGUISTIC MINORITIES

- The formation of this office was prescribed by the States Reorganization Commission.
- This was formed by the Seventh Constitutional Amendment Act of 1956 which inserted a new article 350-B in Part XVII.
- The Special Officer for Linguistic Minorities is appointed by the president.
- The Commissioner has its headquarters at Allahabad with three regional offices at Belgaum, Chennai, and Kolkata.
- The Commissioner is assisted by Deputy Commissioner and an Assistant Commissioner at headquarters.
- The Commissioner falls under the Ministry of Minority Affairs and submits reports to the President through Union Minority Affairs Minister.

Role of the Commissioner:

- All the grievances related to the various safeguards provided for the linguistic minorities are looked into by the Commissioner.
- The Commissioner strives for providing equal opportunities to the linguistic minorities.
- He works for the effective implementation of the various s

Mock Test Mcq

WhatAaap us – 8112096712 for free mock test and online exam free bundle , it is free for every customer who purchase our books .

www.ingramcontent.com/pod-product-compliance
Lightning Source LLC
Chambersburg PA
CBHW051438150726
48000CB00005B/2156